Introduction

Do you play Roblox? Ever wonder where all those games on the Games page come from? They all come from one place – Roblox Studio. You can develop your own Roblox game, too! This book is a great place to learn how to program awesome games in Roblox Studio. It will teach you how to code using the Lua language.

What This Book Covers

Chapter One: Hello World! helps you write your first program.

Chapter Two: Roblox Studio Elements identifies the parts of Roblox Studio.

Chapter Three: Using Scripts teaches you what a Script is and how to use one in your Roblox game.

Chapter Four: Variables shows you how to store data in a Script using code.

Chapter Five: Changing Properties emphasizes how to change the properties of objects in your game world.

Chapter Six: Conditionals focuses on the use of dependent statements.

Chapter Seven: Loops covers loops and repetitive code

Chapter Eight: Day-Night Cycle will be your first project and teach you how to add a cycle between day and night in your game.

Chapter Nine: Functions shows you how you can avoid repeating code by defining and using functions.

Chapter Ten: Tables introduces you to tables, a useful way to store a large amount of data in a single variable.

Chapter Eleven: Project Hierarchy and Comments identifies how your game is set up as well as a way to organize your code.

Chapter Twelve: Color-Changing Brick instructs you on how to make a brick that smoothly changes colors.

Chapter Thirteen: RBXScriptSignal shows how to add listeners to events that occur in the game.

Chapter Fourteen: Instances teaches how to create Parts, Messages, and other game objects through code.

Chapter Fifteen: Humanoids shows how to create characters for your game.

Chapter Sixteen: Values covers values and a way to store values in the game world.

Chapter Seventeen: GUIs shows how to create GUIs (graphical user interfaces) using code, such as buttons, textboxes, labels, etc.

Chapter Eighteen: Tycoon is the final chapter and instructs you on how to create a fully functional tycoon and publish your game on Roblox, allowing your friends to play it.

Part 1

Part 1: Getting Started

Things You Need to Get Started:
- Roblox Studio
- A Windows, Mac OS, Linux, or Chrome OS computer

Note: For the purposes of this book, we will be running Roblox Studio on a Windows 10 computer.

How to Get Roblox Studio (along with Roblox Player):

Roblox Studio comes with Roblox Player when you download and install Roblox. If you do not have Roblox, follow these instructions:

1. Create a Roblox account if you don't already have one
2. Go to the Games page
3. Click on any game
4. Click Play and a popup will be displayed
5. Click Download and Install Roblox
6. Once downloaded, run RobloxPlayerLauncher.exe
7. Install Roblox

Chapter 1: Hello World!

If you're reading this, chances are you want to learn how to create your own Roblox games. Well, you've come to the right place. Ever wonder where all those games on the Games page come from? They were all developed in Roblox Studio. You too can develop your own Roblox games! This book will introduce you to creating games in Roblox Studio. Along the way, you'll enhance your games by coding in the Lua language.

This chapter will cover:

- How to create your first Roblox game

Creating a Game

Once you have Roblox Studio up and running, you should see the following:

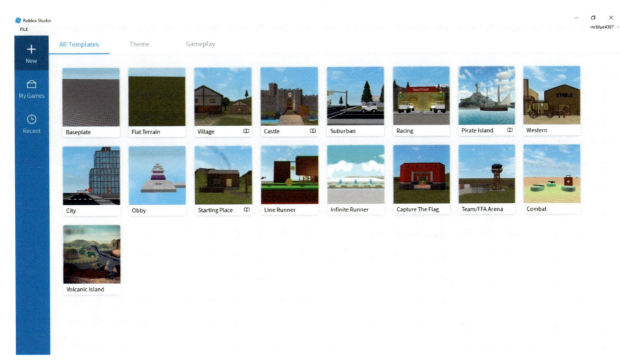

As shown in the picture above, there is a sidebar with 3 buttons – New, My Games, and Recent. The New button allows you to create a new game. My

Games is for managing your games, and Recent is to load recently opened games.

The Roblox Studio start page also shows the game templates you can create, under All Templates. A game template is a starter game to build off of. You should see many templates such as Baseplate, Flat Terrain, Village, Castle, Suburban, and Racing.

To create your first game, click on the New button. Select Baseplate as your first game template. Roblox Studio should load the empty Baseplate as shown in the picture below.

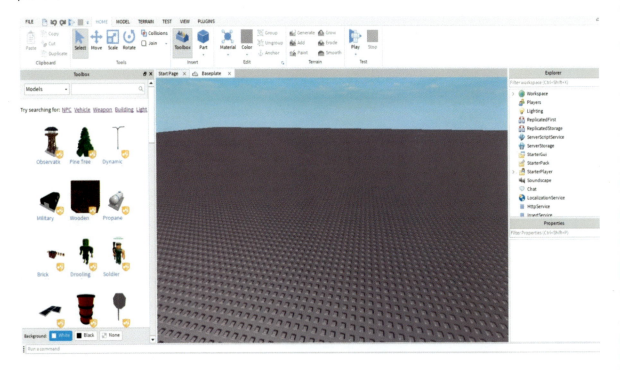

Note: If you do not see the Explorer, Properties, and Toolbox panels, follow these steps:

1. Click on the View menu at the top of the screen.
2. Make sure Explorer, Properties, Toolbox, Command Bar are selected. If they are not already, select them. The results should look similar to the following picture.

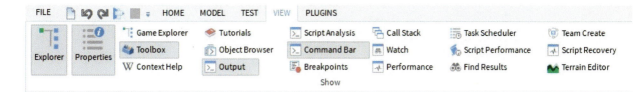

Now that everything is set up, put your mouse in the 3D game window in the Baseplate tab. While holding down the right mouse button, move the cursor. Notice how you can look around. To actually move, use the WASD keys (as you would in Roblox). To zoom in or out, use the mouse wheel. You can also move up and down with the QE keys.

Beginning to Code

To start programming in Roblox Studio, let's use the Command Bar. Click on the View tab and make sure Command Bar and Output are selected.

You should see, at the bottom of the screen, a long text field stretching across the window, as well as an output window.

Roblox Studio uses a programming language called Lua. Lua is a scripting language; if you already have some knowledge of Lua, you won't have a hard time going through this book. However, you do not need any prior knowledge of programming to read this, as this is a beginner's tutorial.

The command bar is where simple lines of code can be entered, and the output window is where the results will be shown.

Start by typing the word `print` in the command bar and an open paren. Then, type "Hello world!" (with the quotes included) and a closed paren. Hit Return and you should see this in the output window:

```
Output
22:38:31.258 - DataModel Loading https://assetgame.roblox.com/Asset/?id=95206881
22:53:25.114 - Baseplate was auto-saved
> print("Hello world!")
Hello world!
```

(If you're wondering, don't pay attention to "Baseplate was auto-saved". This is Roblox Studio saving after a certain interval to make sure the creator doesn't lose progress.)

Hooray! You have run your first command in Roblox Studio. If you didn't see "Hello world!" In the output, double-check your command. It should have looked like this:

```
print("Hello world!")
```

You can also print out numbers. For example, say you wanted to print out some number (fifty-four, for example). You would type

```
print(54)
```

And this would show 54 in the Output window.

Lua is a case-sensitive language. This means that if you accidentally capitalize a letter, then the statement won't work. Also, it is crucial that you include the parentheses around what you want to print. Finally, if you want to print a word or phrase, you must make sure to add quotation marks around the word. They can be single or double quotes, as long as both are of one type.

For example: suppose you wanted to print "Roblox is cool". If you typed

```
print(Roblox is cool)
```

This would be the output:

Page 8

> 23:14:50.690 - Error in script: ')' expected near 'is'

Quotes are extremely important. If you put quotes, the output would show "Roblox is cool!" This is because you can print numbers like 54 or 123.4 without quotes, but you must print strings ("Roblox is cool!") with quotes. You will learn more about this in Chapter 4.

Make sure to save (Ctrl – S) to ensure that you don't lose your changes.

Chapter 2. Introduction to Roblox Studio

This chapter will cover:

- What you can do with Roblox Studio
- The elements of Roblox Studio

The power of Roblox Studio

Roblox Studio is an extremely powerful tool that you can use to create Roblox games. Using Roblox Studio, you can make a tycoon, obby, runner, tower defense game, role-playing game, shooter, and other genres.

Roblox Studio Elements

In Roblox Studio, there are many visual elements. You learned about the Command Bar and Output in the last chapter. But what is the Explorer? The Properties? The Toolbox? Their functions are listed below.

Explorer

The Explorer is a panel on the right where you can view all the components of the game. Click on the caret next to the Workspace icon to open up the workspace. There you will see the Camera, Terrain, and Baseplate.

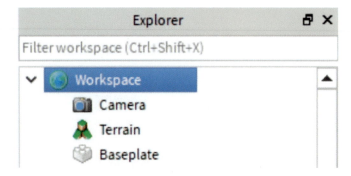

Workspace is the folder where all of the visible components of the game will exist. All bricks that you want to be visible must be in the Workspace.

The Baseplate, under the Workspace, is the wide gray brick that you see. Make sure *not* to delete the Camera or the Baseplate.

The Camera is your point of view in the Roblox Studio virtual world. If you delete it, the game will automatically regenerate it, but your point of view, or where you are looking, will be reset to the center of the Baseplate. If you delete the Baseplate, all players that enter your game will have nothing to spawn on and will fall infinitely, causing them to die repeatedly. You can make it invisible, but it should not be deleted. The Terrain element is, well, the terrain in your game. Rock, grass, or water terrain can be added or generated, but this will not be covered in the book.

There are other folders besides the Workspace, such as Players — the folder where players exist in the game when they enter — Lighting, ReplicatedFirst, and StarterPlayer, but don't worry about those for now. Just remember that all the objects in the workspace are (if possible) shown in the 3D world. Any objects outside of Workspace will not physically interact with the world unless through something in the Workspace.

Properties

Another window on the screen is the Properties panel. The Properties panel shows the properties of objects that you select. For example, click on the Baseplate in the Explorer window under the Workspace.

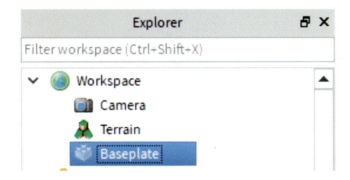

You should see this in the Properties window:

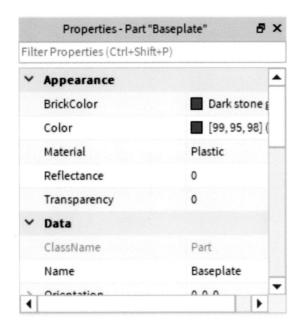

The Properties window shows the properties of the selected object, such as its color, material, reflectance, transparency, name, orientation, etc. Using this window, you could "delete" the Baseplate (by setting its Transparency property to 1.00 and its CanCollide value to false, meaning that you won't be able to touch it or see it when playing), but this is not recommended for testing purposes—doing this would force players to fall through the Baseplate and die indefinitely.

Toolbox

You already know about the Output panel, the Command bar, the Explorer, and the Properties panel. The final area that you might need later on is the Toolbox.

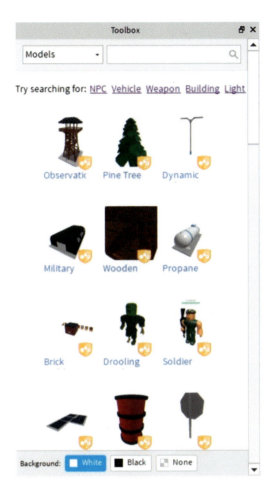

The toolbox window is where you can find free models by searching in the text field at the top. Models are groupings of bricks that can be moved around easily, instead of moving each individual brick. You can also search for audio, decals, and meshes by clicking on the dropdown that says Models. You will learn more about Models later.

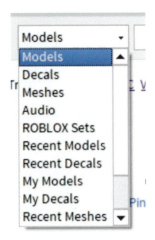

Enter "Car" in the search box and press Return. You should see car-related search results. Click on one, and you should see it in the workspace.

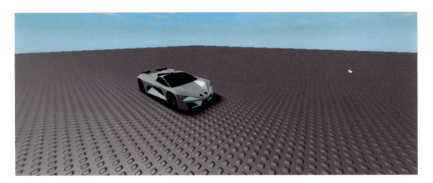

To test your game, click on the button with a character and a triangle in the top of the screen. Through this book, we will refer to it as "Running the game" or "Testing the game", as well as "Playing the game".

Your character should spawn in the center of the Baseplate. Walk into the car, and you might be able to drive it around.

Page 14

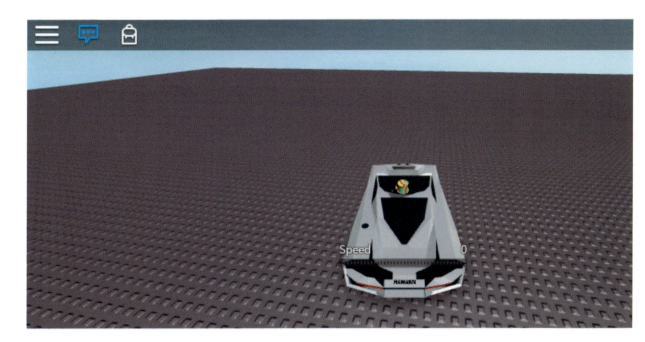

You can use the toolbox to search for any model and put almost anything into your game. However, do make sure to give credit to the original creator of the free model.

Finally, to get back to editing your game, click the red square next to the Play button.

In later chapters, you will learn what you can do with these elements and how they can be interlinked to create an awesome game.

Part 2

Part 2: The Basics

In Part 2, you will learn about the basics of making games on Roblox Studio. Instead of using the command line to run your code, you can use a special object in Roblox Studio called a Script. A Script does anything that the command line can, but instead of running as soon as you press Return, this runs whenever you specify. By default, Scripts execute as soon as the game runs, as opposed to when you are editing the game.

There will be four goals to Part 2. The first is to create a day-night cycle in your Roblox game. The second will be to create a brick that smoothly changes colors. The third goal will be to create a button that makes a cannonball that shoots out of player's heads in the direction they are facing, and the fourth goal is to make a tycoon, which are often featured on the front page of Roblox games. You will use Scripts to achieve these three goals.

Chapter 3. Using Scripts

Scripts

Previously, we used the command bar to feed instructions one at a time. In this chapter, you will learn how you can provide a list of instructions through a Script, which is like a Lua code file where you can type multiple instructions. Each instruction will be executed line by line when the game runs – unlike the command bar, which runs whatever code you entered as soon as you press Return. Scripts can execute as long as they are in a script-running environment such as the Workspace.

Creating a Script

Start by choosing the Model menu at the top of the page, and click on the Part icon.

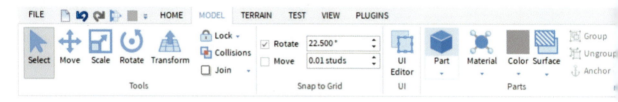

You will see a small, medium-gray brick in the game view, along with a Part object in the Workspace. We will be referring to bricks as Parts in this book because that is what they are called in Roblox.

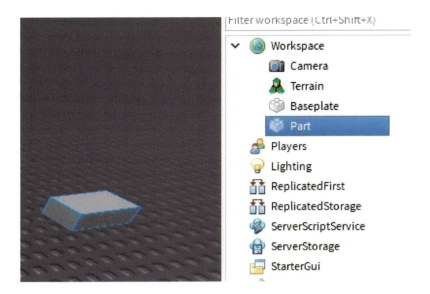

Click on the Part that you have inserted. You should see its properties in the Properties panel. Scroll down until you see the Anchored property. An anchored object will not move around when the game is running unless its Position is changed through a Script. Click the checkbox next to the Anchored property.

Next, insert a script into this part. Right-click the part and choose Insert Object → Script

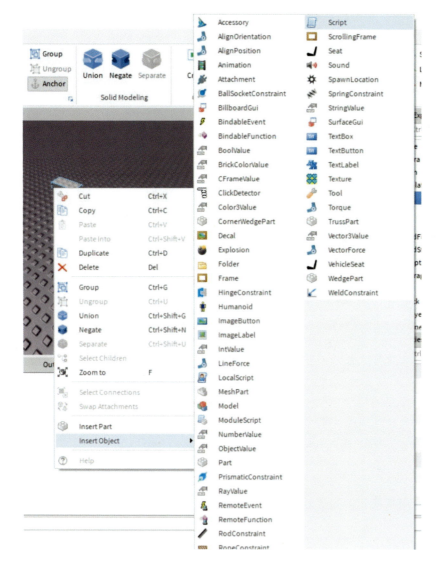

After you insert a script, a new window should pop up. This window is the Script editor and will allow you to write Lua code.

```
print("Hello world!")
```

When you create a new script, Roblox automatically fills it with the text shown above. Run your game and look at the output. You should see

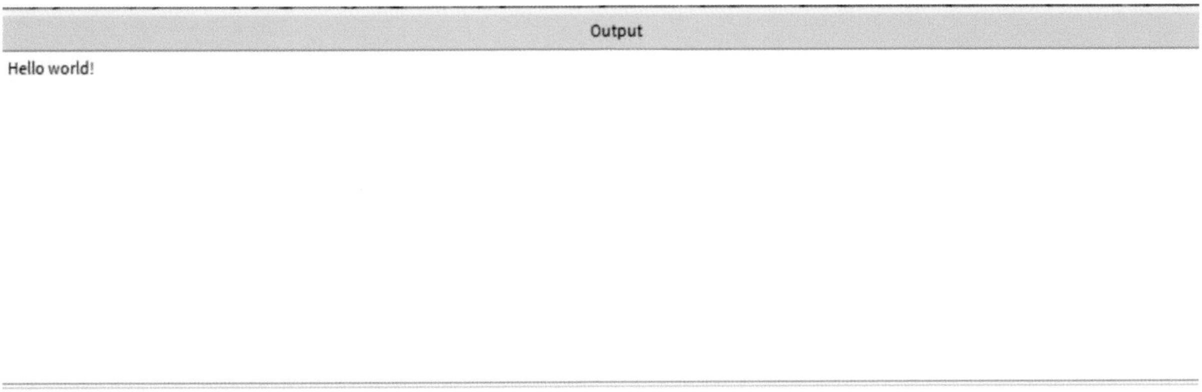

Output
Hello world!

Scripts do not have to be inside a Part. Delete your Part by clicking on it and pressing Delete, or by right-clicking the Part and selecting Delete. Then, right-click on Workspace and hover over Insert Object → Script.

You should see the text in the picture above in the editor again. Run your game and view the output. It should say "Hello world!", as it did when you put the Script in a Part.

Chapter 4. Variables

What is a Variable?

In programming, variables are used to temporarily store values so you can use them later on. To use them, you just have to refer to the variable's name; this makes it so you don't have to retype the value each time you want to access it.

Open up a previous script (or make a new one) and delete all the code.

If you run your game now, there will be no output (unless you have other Scripts) as there is nothing in your Script yet.

Using variables is easy. Type `local i = 0` in your Script. This will be explained in a moment.

```
local i = 0
```

Creating a variable is known as *declaring* a variable. In this example, you are declaring the variable **i** and setting its value, as the equal sign is equivalent to "This variable's value will be whatever is on the right side of the equals sign."

You can also omit the `local`, but it is not required. Also, Roblox Studio will complain. Why? There are two basic types of variables – local and global variables. This will be discussed in detail later in the chapter.

If you run your game, nothing happens yet. To use the variable, add a print statement in your Script.

```
local i = 0
print(i)
```

Run the game, and view the output. You should see 0 printed.

```
Output
0
```

When the interpreter sees the `local i = 0` keyword, it creates a new variable with the name of `i` and sets it to the value after the equals sign. `local` means that the variable can be accessed only by code inside that block. A block is a structure of code which is grouped together, usually under control structures such as loops or conditionals, which you will learn more about later. If you didn't have the `local`

You can go back into your Script and change the value of `i` to whatever you want. I will change it to "Roblox". The output will be "Roblox".

As I mentioned, variables can be changed. Copy the following into your Script:

```
local i = "Roblox"
print(i)
i = "IS AWESOME!"
print(i)
```

Run your game, and you should see two lines of output.

```
Output                                    □ ×
Roblox
IS AWESOME
```

Because you already declared the variable (`local i = 0`), you don't have to add another `local` when changing its value.

Variable Math

You can also do basic math on variables and numbers. For example, if you had a variable called **variable** with a value of **5**, `print(variable * 5)` would output 25. Here are the arithmetic operators you can use on variables:

Operator	Definition	Example	
+	Plus	5 + 4	9
-	Minus	5 - 4	1
*	Multiplied by	5 * 4	20
/	Divided by	5 / 4	1.25
^	To the power of	5 ^ 4	625
%	Mod (remainder when divided)	5 % 4	1

If your variable is a boolean value (**true** or **false**), you can use these operators.

Operator	Definition	Example	
And	Both values are true	true and true	True
Or	One of the values is true	false or true	True
Not	Opposite of value	not true	False

There are some rules to remember when naming a variable. For example:

- You can't put spaces in variable names
    - You can capitalize the letter of the second word
    - You can put an underscore (Shift-dash) instead of a space

- You can't start variable names with a number
- You can't use characters such as the following *anywhere* in a variable name:
    - ~`!?@#$%^&*(){}[]\|/;:'",.<>
- You can't use Lua keywords as variable names:
    - **and, end, in, repeat, break, false, local, return, do, for, nil, then, else, function, not, true, elseif, if, or, until, while**
- Don't name variables the same name as a function

Don't name a variable `print`, for example, because then `print(...)` will not work as you would expect it to.

Local Explanation

Each piece of code that Lua executes, such as a Script or a single line in the command bar, is called a chunk. The `local` keyword means that the variable to be declared is local to that chunk. Once every line in the chunk has finished executing, the variable will be inaccessible. For example, type `local a = "A"` in the command bar. Then, press Return. Try `print(a)`. Because `a` was from another chunk (that one line of code) it cannot be accessed. How would you fix this? Type `a = "A"` and press Return. When typing the next command, you can use `print(a)` and it will work. You must remove the local in the command bar. Another workaround is to type all the code in one line.

```
local i = 50 print(i)
```

This code is very hard to read. This is the purpose of a Script – to fit numerous lines of code without ugly formatting.

After typing the statement, hit Return and you should see 50 printed in the Output window.

Why The Quotes?

There are seven datatypes in Lua. Each datatype is, obviously, a type of data, and can be applied to a variable. They are as follows: nil, booleans, numbers, strings, tables, functions, and userdata/threads. Nil is a concept of the absence of a value. It is the default value of all variables. Booleans are the true/false variable values. Numbers are, of course, numbers. Strings are like words or phrases—"strings" of characters. Tables and functions you will learn later in the book. Userdata and threading are much more complicated and will not be covered. Userdata represent datatypes in the underlying C program. Each of these datatypes can be represented by a variable. For example, a variable can be assigned to nil, booleans, numbers, strings, tables, functions, and userdata/threads.

Chapter 5. Changing Properties

The Properties of a Part

To understand this chapter, you must first select the Baseplate (under Workspace in the Explorer) and view the properties. Try changing the material of the Baseplate to Fabric. You should see something like this:

For now, change it back to plastic.

So, what if you wanted to do this through code? To change a property of an object, you would have to have a variable assigned to it and type, `<variable>.Material = Enum.Material.Fabric`. `Enum`s are arrays of already-set values that you can use by typing `Enum.<enumName>.<enumValue>`. Here, you set the Material property of the baseplate to `Enum.Material.Fabric`.

Try it! Create a new script (or open one that you have already created) and type this:

```
local baseplate = workspace.Baseplate
baseplate.Material = Enum.Material.Fabric
```

Let's run through this code before we test it.

At line one, we get a variable to the Baseplate called `baseplate`. `workspace.Baseplate` means to get the Baseplate from the `workspace` folder, and since it is on the right of an equals sign, it is assigned to the `baseplate` variable.

At line two, we set the Material property of the variable to `Enum.Material.Fabric`.

If you run your game, you should see that the Baseplate's material became `Fabric`.

Suppose you had a Part whose parent was the Baseplate. (Yes, that is possible. In fact, if you want to do that, right-click on the Baseplate in the explorer, click Insert Part, and, using the explorer, drag the Part into the Baseplate.) If you wanted to change a property (such as the Transparency), you would use this code:

```
local part = workspace.Baseplate.Part
part.Transparency = 0.5
```

You could also make it shorter by typing this:

```
workspace.Baseplate.Part.Transparency = 0.5
```

As you may have noticed, Parts have a BrickColor property. You can create a new BrickColor by calling `BrickColor.new(<colorName>)` So, to change the color of the baseplate, you can use this code:

```
workspace.Baseplate.BrickColor = BrickColor.new("Cyan")
```

Running the game will show a cyan baseplate.

To see all the possible colors you could put in BrickColor.new("..."), select the Baseplate, and click on the BrickColor value in the Properties panel. You should see a popup that allows you to select the color of the Baseplate. Hover over one color; Roblox should should tell you what the color name is of that color. If you click on that color, the Baseplate's color will change to it.

You can also use one of the preset colors. To use this, simply type `BrickColor.Blue()` or `BrickColor.Red()`. If you have basic knowledge of RGB colors, you can use `BrickColor.fromRGB(r,g,b)`. You then replace `r`, `g`, and `b` with the red, green, and blue values respectively (1-256).
`BrickColor.new(r,g,b)` can also be used, but the red, green, and blue values have to be from 0-1. The final option to use is `BrickColor.Random()`, which returns a random value each time it is used.

Chapter 6. Conditionals

If-Then-Else

Arguably the most fundamental part of programming is the `if` statement. An `if` statement is a block of code that runs when a certain declared condition is met. This is the format of an `if` statement:

```
local condition = true
if condition then

end
```

Here is an example of an `if` statement:

```
local name = "John"
if name == "John" then
    print("The name is John!")
end
```

Note that in the `if` statement above, we use a double-equals sign (`==`) to make sure that the two values are equal.

If you run the game, you should see "The name is John!" printed in the Output panel.

What if the name value *isn't* John? This is called an `else` statement. Here is an example:

```
local name = "Joe Bob"
if name == "John" then
    print("Hi, John!")
else
    print("The name is "..name.."!")
end
```

Notice the `..` At line two. This is an operator in Lua that concatenates the strings on both sides of it. If you run your game, you should see "The name is Joe Bob!" in the output.

What if you wanted to check if the name was Julia if it was not John? You could put another `if` statement in the else block, but there is another, less complicated, and more readable solution—the `elseif` keyword. The `elseif` keyword is similar to `if` except for the fact that all `elseif`s need an `if`. If the `if` condition is false, the interpreter will check the `elseif` condition. If you do not understand, you will in a moment. View the code snippet below.

```
local name = "John"
if name == "John" then
    print("Hi, John!")
elseif name == "Julia" then
    print("Hi, Julia!")
else
    print("The name is "..name.."!")
end
```

If you run your game, you should see "Hi, Julia!" In the output.

You can compare other things, too, such as BrickColors. This example compares the Baseplate's BrickColor with the Dark Stone Grey BrickColor.

```
local baseplate = workspace.Baseplate
if baseplate.BrickColor == BrickColor.new("Dark stone grey") then
    print("The Baseplate's BrickColor is Dark stone grey")
else
    print("The Baseplate's BrickColor is not Dark stone grey")
end
```

Instead of a double-equals sign, you can compare two values with these operators:

Operator	Definition	Example	
<	Less than	1 < 3	True
>	Greater than	1 > 3	False
<=	Less than or equal to	3 <= 5	True
>=	Greater than or equal to	3 >= 5	False
==	Is equal to	3 == 5	False
~=	Is not equal to	3 ~= 5	True

Nil Checks

You learned about `nil` in Chapter 4. `nil` is the absence of a value – the equivalent of null or None in other languages.

So how would you check if a variable is equal to `nil`? There is a special type of if-statement called a nil check. The format is like this:

```
local variable = nil
if variable then
    print("It's not nil!")
else
    print("It's nil!")
end
```

The output is what you might expect:

```
It's nil!
```

This is because if the variable is nil, then the `if variable then` condition is false. If the variable is *not* nil, then the `if variable then` condition is true.

Chapter 7. Looping

While Loops

Another important part of programming is a loop. A loop is a block of code that runs while a condition is true. Loops are useful in situations when you want to repeat a line (or lines) of code without having to type them all out. If you don't understand, don't worry – you will in a moment.

One common type of loop is a while loop. The format of a while loop goes like this:

```
local variable = true
while variable do

end
```

To shorten it, you could take out the first line and replace **variable** on line two with **true**. However, do *not* run this—this is an infinite loop, and if you do not add a wait statement inside it, Roblox Studio will crash. To prevent this, add **wait(0.2)** between the beginning of the **while** loop and the **end**.

```
local variable = true
while variable do
    wait(0.2)
end
```

Now, when you run the game, nothing will happen. You haven't added anything in the **while** loop yet. Let's change this.

Suppose you wanted to change the color of the Baseplate every half second to a random color. You would get a reference to the Baseplate, and set its BrickColor value to **BrickColor.Random()**. Here is how to do it in code:

```
local baseplate = script.Parent.Baseplate
while true do
    baseplate.BrickColor = BrickColor.Random()
    wait(0.5)
end
```

Have you noticed that I introduced something new? The **script** keyword refers to the script that it is in. **script.Parent** means, "Go to the direct parent of this script." Since I put this script in the Workspace, **script.Parent.Baseplate** is saying, "Find the parent of this script (in this case Workspace) and look for a child called Baseplate".

Run your game and view your disco Baseplate.

If you wanted to make it flash colors faster, shorten the delay in wait(). For example, you could change it to 0.3 and see the colors flash more frequently.

For Loops

What if you wanted the baseplate to flash random colors, but only twenty times? You would use a `for` loop. Here is the code:

```lua
local baseplate = script.Parent.Baseplate
for variable = 1, 20, 1 do
    baseplate.BrickColor = BrickColor.Random()
    wait(0.5)
end
```

At line one, we get a variable to the Baseplate with `script.Parent.Baseplate`. At line two, we create a `for` loop. `for` loops go like this: `for <variable> = 1, <timesToRepeat>, <step> do`. So, in this code, `variable` is set to one at the beginning (note there doesn't need to be a local), and the step is 1. Here is an an explanation:

1. Create a variable called `variable` and set its value to `1`.
2. Execute this code while `variable` is not twenty.
3. After each iteration, increment `variable` by `1`.

I added a `wait()` call in this code so our eyes can process the color-changing. Computers can run code very quickly, so without a `wait` call (which forces the Script to wait), you would only see the final color.

Run your code and view your disco Baseplate, but after twenty colors, it should stop.

You can remove the second comma and the second one in the for-loop; the default step in a `Lua` for loop is one.

```lua
local baseplate = script.Parent.Baseplate
for variable = 1, 20 do
    baseplate.BrickColor = BrickColor.Random()
    wait(0.3)
end
```

Repeat-Until Loops

A **repeat ... until ...** statement will repeat until a condition is true. The body is executed at least once, because the condition is tested after the body executes.

```
local i = 0
repeat
    print("i is " , i)
    wait(0.2)
    i = i + 1
until i > 10
```

The output will be

```
i is 0
i is 1
i is 2
i is 3
i is 4
i is 5
i is 6
i is 7
i is 8
i is 9
i is 10
```

First, we declared a variable called **i**. Then, we printed the value of **i** and waited **0.2** seconds and incremented **i**. The loop repeated this until the variable **i** became **11**. Because **i** was then greater than **10**, the loop stopped.

Break

If you had an infinite loop you can end it with a **break** statement. You can also use **break** statements in loops that are not infinite. For example:

```
for var = 30, 10, -2 do
    print(var)
    if var == 14 then
        break
    end
end
```

The **break** statement can go in any type of loop. This **for** loop prints out all the numbers from thirty to fourteen that are divisible by two.

Page 35

```
30
28
26
24
22
20
18
16
14
```

Chapter 8. Day/Night Cycle

Lighting

If you have played advanced Roblox games in the past, you may have noticed that the time of day changes. The service that controls the time of day is called Lighting. In the Explorer panel, you should see Lighting just under Players. Lighting has a function called `SetMinutesAfterMidnight`; we can use this to specify the exact time of day.

Start by inserting a script into the Workspace and deleting the default code.

Now, we are going to do something different. There is a root element known as `game`. The game element is hidden, but it is the parent of the Workspace, Players, Lighting, etc. So, to use the `SetMinutesAfterMidnight` function, type this code:

```lua
local hoursAfterMidnight = 8
game.Lighting:SetMinutesAfterMidnight(hoursAfterMidnight * 60)
```

Try changing around the value to whatever hour you want it to be.

Changing the time of day once isn't that useful. Let's create a loop that changes the time of day infinitely and waits.

Encase line two in a `while-true-do` loop. After you set the time of day, increment `hoursAfterMidnight` by `1` and wait for one second.

```lua
local hoursAfterMidnight = 8
while true do
    game.Lighting:SetMinutesAfterMidnight(hoursAfterMidnight * 60)
    hoursAfterMidnight = hoursAfterMidnight + 1
    wait(1)
end
```

You may have noticed that the sun and moon seem to teleport across the sky. To fix this, remove `hoursAfterMidnight` and replace it with `minsAfterMidnight`. Tweak the numbers a little bit and see what works best for you. Personally, I think this is very smooth:

```
local minsAfterMidnight = 8*60
while true do
    game.Lighting:SetMinutesAfterMidnight(minsAfterMidnight)
    minsAfterMidnight = minsAfterMidnight + 0.5
    wait(0.05)
end
```

And voilà! You now have a day/night cycle.

Note: In `game.Lighting:SetMinutesAfterMidnight`, the colon denotes that `SetMinutesAfterMidnight` is a method. A method is a special type of function that is usually used in OOP (object-oriented programming.) Calling `game.Lighting: SetMinutesAfterMidnight(mins)` is the same as calling `game.Lighting. SetMinutesAfterMidnight(game.Lighting, mins)`

Chapter 9. Functions

Functions

Functions are ways of grouping code so that it can be reused repeatedly. We have used many functions previously, such as `BrickColor.New()`, `BrickColor.Random()`, `SetMinutesAfterMidnight(minutes)`, and `print()`. All functions have three parts:

- The function name (such as print)
- The parentheses
- The parameters

What are parameters? Parameters, also known as arguments, are variables that you pass into the function. For example, the `print` function takes in as many arguments as you want. However, `BrickColor.Random()` takes none.

To define a function, you have to type `function <functionNameHere>(<params>)` and close it with an `end`. You can also add a local since all functions are variables. For example:

```
local function myFunc(value)
    print(value)
end

myFunc("hi")
myFunc("HELLOOO")
```

At lines 1-3, you define a function that takes in a value and `print`s it. Then, you call that function twice with different values. You should see those values in the output.

Functions can take anything as another value, such as other functions:

```
local function doSomething(otherFunc)
    otherFunc("From doSomething()")
end

local function myFunction(value)
    print(value.." from myFunction()")
end

doSomething(myFunction)
```

`doSomething()` takes in a value and passes "From `doSomething()`" to that value. It happened to be `myFunction()`, which appended " `from myFunction()`" to it and printed it. The result is "From doSomething() from myFunction()"

What if you wanted to do something other than create and call your own functions? For example, you could clone an already existing Part in the Workspace using functions. Here is how:

Insert a part into the Workspace by right-clicking on the Workspace and clicking Insert Part, or by clicking on the Part icon in the Model tab. Change its BrickColor to another color. Then, select the part in the Explorer and press F2. Rename the part "CloneObject". Open your script (or insert one into the Workspace) and delete all the code. You will get a reference to the Part you inserted and clone it:

```
local function clone()
    local clonePart = script.Parent.CloneObject
    local clone = clonePart:Clone()
    clone.Parent = workspace
end

while true do
    clone()
    wait(1)
end
```

Run your code; you should see many Parts in the workspace.

Chapter 10. Tables

What are Tables?

Tables are useful for storing multiple objects, such as variables, Parts, etc. You can iterate through tables and get each value individually instead of typing out the variable name.

```lua
local myNumbers = {1, 2, 3, 4, 5}
```

If you are familiar with other programming languages, you may notice that tables are similar to arrays. Tables are the Lua equivalent of arrays and lists (and dictionaries).

To retrieve a value at an index from a table, use **table[index]**. For example:

```lua
local myNumbers = {1, 2, 3, 4, 5}
print(myNumbers[1])
print(myNumbers[3])
```

Because **1** is at the first position in the table, **print(myNumbers[1])** will output the element at index **1**, which is **1**.

Iteration

If you had a long table of elements and wanted to print each one, you could use a loop and print out the value at each index in the table. However, there is a simpler method—the **pairs(table)** function.

For example, suppose you had a table like this:

```lua
local alphabet = {"A", "B", "C", "D", "E", "F", "G", "H", "I", "J", "K", "L", "M",
    "N", "O", "P", "Q", "R", "S", "T", "U", "V", "W", "X", "Y", "Z"
}
```

You would iterate through this using the **pairs(table)** function.

pairs() takes in a table as a parameter and returns the indexes and values in the table. For this reason, I like to use **pairs()** like this:

```lua
local alphabet = {"A", "B", "C", "D", "E", "F", "G", "H", "I", "J", "K", "L", "M",
    "N", "O", "P", "Q", "R", "S", "T", "U", "V", "W", "X", "Y", "Z"
}
for i,v in pairs(alphabet) do
    print("The element at index "..i.." is "..v)
end
```

To see how many items are in a table, add a pound sign (`#`) before it.

```lua
local alphabet = {"A", "B", "C", "D", "E", "F", "G", "H", "I", "J", "K", "L", "M",
    "N", "O", "P", "Q", "R", "S", "T", "U", "V", "W", "X", "Y", "Z"
}
print("The length of alphabet is "..#alphabet)
```

If you do not use `pairs()` and try to print your table, it will output the unique id of the table.

Table Altering

To add values to a table, you can use `table.insert(table, newValue)` or `table[#table + 1] = newValue`. The second method takes the size of the table and adds one. Then, it uses this to append an element to the end of the table. To insert an element at a certain index in the table, use `table.insert(table, yourIndex, newValue)` or `table[index] = newValue`.

To remove a value, you can use `table.remove(table, index)`

Sorting a table can be done with `table.sort()`, which does so in natural sort order (1, 2, 3, 4, 5; a, b, c, d, e).

Finally, `table.concat(table, string)` returns a string, which is a "string" of characters. (Need a recap? Go to the end of Chapter 4.) In the string is each value of your table, but with the second argument between them. For example:

```lua
local t = {"A", "B", "C", "D", "E", "F"}
local str = table.concat(t, " < ")

print(str)
```

This would output

Output
A<B<C<D<E<F

Table Sorting

You can sort a table in Lua using the `table.sort(table)` function. Here is an example.

```lua
t = {8, 3, 5, 1, 9, 7, 4, 6, 2, 10}
table.sort(t)
for i,v in pairs(t) do
    print(v)
end
```

What does this do? At line 1, a table is created with numbers 1-10 in random order. At line three, the table is sorted. From lines 5-7, each element is printed. You should see the sorted elements of the table in the Output.

String Keys

So far, we have used numbers as indices – or keys – in our table. (Think of it as having several keys. If you put one into your table, you unlock its value.) What if we wanted to use a string – or a word – as a key in our table? You could do it like this:

```
local t = {A = 1,
    B = 2,
    C = 3,
    D = 4,
    E = 5,
    F = 6
}

for i,v in pairs(t) do
    print(i,v)
end
```

The above code would output:

Any string key will work as long as you can use it as a variable name. This, for example, would not work:

```
local t = {foo bar = 123}
```

Because `foo bar` is not a valid variable name.

Chapter 11. Game Hierarchy & Comments

Hierarchy

The most important part of game design is the hierarchy. This is because every element in your Roblox game is connected to the hierarchy in some form. At the top level is a hidden object called game. It is the parent of all the containers you see in the Explorer—Workspace, Players, Lighting, etc. You can refer to a child by:

```
child = parent.child
child = parent["child"]
child = parent:FindFirstChild("child")
```

Using these methods, you can reference Players by simply using `game.Players`. The first two will cause an error if there is no child by that exact name (`"child"`). The third will return `nil`, which is the Lua version of null, or nothing. Here is an example:

```
local baseplate1 = workspace.Baseplate
local baseplate2 = workspace["Baseplate"]
local baseplate3 = workspace:FindFirstChild("Baseplate")

print(baseplate1 == baseplate2)
print(baseplate2 == baseplate3)
```

You can also move back up the tree using `child.Parent.Parent` etc. Until you find the correct element. You can also use `child.Parent.otherChild` to locate a sibling of the object.

More Tables

To find all children of an element in the Roblox game hierarchy, use

```
local element = workspace

for i,v in pairs(element:GetChildren()) do
    print(v.Name)
end
```

`GetChildren()` returns a table of the children of that element; note that you must use a colon before `GetChildren()`, and it only works on elements in the game hierarchy. Same with the child references as shown above – they will not work on elements outside of the game hierarchy. For example, it would not be possible to use these on variables because they are not in the game hierarchy.

Comments

A comment is a programmer-readable explanation or annotation in the source code of a computer program. They are added to make the code easier for humans to understand and are generally ignored by compilers and interpreters, which are the parts of the computer that read in the Lua code and turn it into stuff the computer can understand.

You could add comments to all of your Scripts saying, "This is what this does: …" and Roblox will not care about these lines.

To use comments, type `--`. You can type anything after that, and the Script will ignore it. You can put code or your own text there, and it will be skipped. For multiline comments, use `--[[` to begin one and `]]` to end one.

```lua
local topSecret = "CLASSIFIED"
print(topSecret) -- Outputs "CLASSIFIED"
```

That was a single-line comment. This is an example of a multiline comment:

```lua
print("Before a multi-line comment")

--[[
    This is an example of a multiline comment
    skip
    skip
    See? It's still a comment!
]]

print("After a multi-line comment")
```

Chapter 12. Color-Changing Brick

Linear Interpolation

Recall in Chapter 7 that you created a color-changing Baseplate through code. You may have noticed that the change from color to color was not smooth. In this chapter, you will put all that you learned together to create a smoothly color-changing Part. Here's how: Linear interpolation (abbreviated as `lerp`) is a useful tool in Roblox Studio that returns a value between two set values. You can use this to gradually transition between colors. For example, to make the change between red and blue seem gradual, you could add a color to change to in the middle – a violet color. `lerp`ing is used in animation to show smoothly transition from one frame to another.

The bare bones code of a color-changing Part is like this: (keep in mind that this Script is inside the Part that you want to smoothly change color)

```
local part = script.Parent

local function changeColor()

end

while true do
    changeColor()
end
```

Using what you learned in Chapter 10, we can create a table of the colors that we want the Part to transition to.

```
local part = script.Parent

local red = Color3.new(1, 0, 0)              -- 100% red
local orange = Color3.new(1, 0.5, 0)         -- 100% red, 50% green
local yellow = Color3.new(1, 1, 0)           -- 100% red, 100% green
local green = Color3.new(0, 1, 0)            -- 100% green
local blue = Color3.new(0, 0, 1)             -- 100% blue
local indigo = Color3.new(0.25, 0.125, 0.5)  -- 25% red, 12.5% green, 50% blue
local violet = Color3.new(0.5, 0.25, 0.5)    -- 50% red, 25% green, 50% blue

local function changeColor()

end

while true do
    changeColor()
end
```

I will be making mine a rainbow color-changing brick. From lines 3-9, what we are doing is basically defining the color variables for every color in the rainbow. We then put the color values into a table of colors.

If you don't want to use the rainbow colors, you can look up the RGB (red, green, blue) values of the colors that you want to use. For example, if you wanted to use brown instead of orange, you could look up "Brown RGB" and find its RGB value. Instead of using `Color3.new(r, g, b)` (which takes in decimal values between 0 and 1 as parameters), you could use `Color3.fromRGB(r, g, b)` (which takes in numbers from 0-256 as red, green, and blue values). So, to use brown, you would use this code:

```lua
local part = script.Parent

local red = Color3.new(1, 0, 0)              -- 100% red
local brown = Color3.fromRGB(165, 42, 42)
local yellow = Color3.new(1, 1, 0)           -- 100% red, 100% green
local green = Color3.new(0, 1, 0)            -- 100% green
local blue = Color3.new(0, 0, 1)             -- 100% blue
local indigo = Color3.new(0.25, 0.125, 0.5)  -- 25% red, 12.5% green, 50% blue
local violet = Color3.new(0.5, 0.25, 0.5)    -- 50% red, 25% green, 50% blue

local function changeColor()

end

while true do
    changeColor()
end
```

And then you would replace orange in the table of colors with brown.

Moving on, let's actually change the color of the Part. To do this, we loop through a table of colors (in the order that we want the colors to show) and change the color of the Part to each color, and then wait.

```
local part = script.Parent

local red = Color3.new(1, 0, 0)              -- 100% red
local orange = Color3.new(1, 0.5, 0)         -- 100% red, 50% green
local yellow = Color3.new(1, 1, 0)           -- 100% red, 100% green
local green = Color3.new(0, 1, 0)            -- 100% green
local blue = Color3.new(0, 0, 1)             -- 100% blue
local indigo = Color3.new(0.25, 0.125, 0.5)  -- 25% red, 12.5% green, 50% blue
local violet = Color3.new(0.5, 0.25, 0.5)    -- 50% red, 25% green, 50% blue

local colors = {red, orange, yellow, green, indigo, violet}

local function changeColor()
    for index,color in pairs(colors) do
        part.Color = color
        wait(0.1)
    end
end

while true do
    changeColor()
end
```

This is it, right? Is this a color-changing Part? Yes. Is it a *smoothly* color-changing Part? No. We can fix that with `color:lerp()`, or linear interpolation.

How does the `color:lerp(endColor, interval)` method work? It takes in two parameters – the `endColor` and the `interval`. What does this mean? Suppose you told somebody, "Give me a number halfway between zero and one." You would get 0.5. If you said, "Give me a number 10 percent between zero and one," you would get 0.1. This is like linear interpolation. You have the start color and the end color – if you want to smoothly transition between the two colors, you would, for example, change the color to 10 percent between the two colors; then 20 percent; then 30 percent; etc. until it reaches 100 percent. Then you begin changing the color 10, 20, 30, 40, … percent toward the next color.

```lua
local part = script.Parent

local red = Color3.new(1, 0, 0)              -- 100% red
local orange = Color3.new(1, 0.5, 0)         -- 100% red, 50% green
local yellow = Color3.new(1, 1, 0)           -- 100% red, 100% green
local green = Color3.new(0, 1, 0)            -- 100% green
local blue = Color3.new(0, 0, 1)             -- 100% blue
local indigo = Color3.new(0.25, 0.125, 0.5)  -- 25% red, 12.5% green, 50% blue
local violet = Color3.new(0.5, 0.25, 0.5)    -- 50% red, 25% green, 50% blue

local colors = {red, orange, yellow, green, indigo, violet}

local function changeColor()
    for index,color in pairs(colors) do
        local startColor = part.Color
        
        for i = 1, 10 do
            local newColor = startColor:lerp(color, i / 10) -- Get 10% closer to
                                                            -- the new color
            part.Color = newColor
            wait(0.05)
        end
        
        wait(0.1)
    end
end

while true do
    changeColor()
end
```

If you think there isn't enough time in the intervals, you can tweak the `wait()` time. You can also create an `intervals` variable at the top of the Script and replace the `10` in the `for` loop and the `lerp()` with intervals. The first `for` loop in `changeColor()` loops through all the colors in the table, and the second `for` loop (inside the first) is for transitioning from one color to the next. You can also set the Material of the Part to Neon for a cool effect.

```lua
local part = script.Parent
local intervals = 40

local red = Color3.new(1, 0, 0)            -- 100% red
local orange = Color3.new(1, 0.5, 0)       -- 100% red, 50% green
local yellow = Color3.new(1, 1, 0)         -- 100% red, 100% green
local green = Color3.new(0, 1, 0)          -- 100% green
local blue = Color3.new(0, 0, 1)           -- 100% blue
local indigo = Color3.new(0.25, 0.125, 0.5) -- 25% red, 12.5% green, 50% blue
local violet = Color3.new(0.5, 0.25, 0.5)  -- 50% red, 25% green, 50% blue

local colors = {red, orange, yellow, green, indigo, violet}

local function changeColor()
    for index,color in pairs(colors) do
        local startColor = part.Color
        
        for i = 1, intervals do
            local newColor = startColor:lerp(color, i / intervals) -- Get 10% closer to
                                                                    -- the new color
            part.Color = newColor
            wait(0.04)
        end
        
        wait(0.1)
    end
end

while true do
    changeColor()
end
```

I tweaked a bit and the result is shown above. I believe it looks very smooth.

Chapter 13. RBXScriptSignal

Events

So far, what we have done in code is pretty useful. However, we have not yet learned how to detect if something touches a Part. This is a vital element in most Roblox games. In this chapter, you will learn how to detect this using an RBXScriptSignal – more commonly known as an *event* – and hook it to a listener to detect when the event is fired. You can do many things with events. You can detect if a Part was touched (which we will be doing in this chapter), if a part was clicked (which we will also be doing), if a Property of an object was changed, if a child was added to an object, and many more.

The Object Browser

To find the full list of Roblox object events, click on the View menu at the top of the screen. Then, click on Object Browser. You should see a new window show up that shows you a list of objects on the left and their properties in the middle.

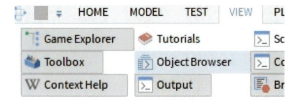

Fundamentals of Scripting with Events

```
local baseplate = workspace.Baseplate

local function onBaseplateTouched(whatTouchedBaseplate)
    print(whatTouchedBaseplate.Name .. " touched the Baseplate!")
end

baseplate.Touched:Connect(onBaseplateTouched)
```

Simple? Yes. The only part that is new is line 7. `Touched` is an event and a property of every Part. It is fired when anything touches a Part. You take the `Touched`

Page 52

event of the Baseplate and `Connect()` it to the function that you made, `onBaseplateTouched(whatTouchedBaseplate)`.

Anonymous Functions

It is possible to use something called an anonymous function when scripting with events. An anonymous function is basically something that you pass in as a parameter to an event that is called when the event fires. You can create an anonymous function like so:

```lua
workspace.Baseplate.Touched:Connect(function(hit)
    workspace.Baseplate.BrickColor = BrickColor.Random()
end)
```

Notice how at line 1, you simply hook a generic function to the `Touched` event. You don't have to give the function a name; you simply type `function(hit)`. `hit` is the object that touched the Baseplate. You can call it anything you want.

Debounce

You may have noticed that the Baseplate continuously flashes random colors when you walk on it. We can fix that using something called debounce. Debounce is a kind of toggleable flag that you can use to determine if the baseplate should change color:

```lua
local debounce = true    -- Whether or not the Baseplate's
                         -- color can be changed

workspace.Baseplate.Touched:Connect(function(hit)
    if debounce then           -- If you can change the color
        debounce = false       -- You can't change the color
        workspace.Baseplate.BrickColor = BrickColor.Random()
        wait(0.5)
        debounce = true        -- You can change the color now
    end
end)
```

Why do you have to use debounce? Why can't we just add a wait call? Because when a Part is touched, the Roblox physics engine sends off multiple messages to each event handler. Each event handler (in your case, the listener that you defined) is called individually and simultaneously, which is why we have to use debounce. Debounce is a way for multiple event listeners to communicate with each other (in a way) and make sure that only one of them runs.

Part Button

There is a special Roblox object called a ClickDetector that has an event which fires when a player clicks on it. It can be used like this:

```lua
local button = script.Parent
local clickDetector = button.ClickDetector

local debounce = true

clickDetector.MouseClick:Connect(function(player)
    if debounce then
        debounce = false

        print(player.Name .. " clicked the button.")
        button.BrickColor = BrickColor.Red()

        wait(0.5)
        debounce = true

        button.BrickColor = BrickColor.Green()
    end
end)
```

The code above will work as long as the Script is placed inside a Part and that Part also has a ClickDetector child.

Player Cannon

Using a ClickDetector, we can create a button that shoots a cannonball out of a player's head when clicked.

Start by inserting a Part into the workspace. From there, insert a ClickDetector into the Part, and then insert a Script into the Part.

We can start by creating a function for shooting the cannonball:

```lua
local function shoot(origin)

end
```

Origin will be where the cannonball originates from. This makes the function more flexible and versatile, for example when we want to shoot the cannonball from somewhere else besides a player's head.

Now we can add the part that creates a cannonball:

```lua
local function shoot(origin)
    local cannonball = Instance.new("Part")
    cannonball.Shape = Enum.PartType.Ball
    cannonball.Velocity = origin.CFrame.lookVector * 300 + Vector3.new(0, 30, 0)
    cannonball.CFrame = origin.CFrame + Vector3.new(0, 2, 0)
    cannonball.Size = Vector3.new(1.5, 1.5, 1.5)
    cannonball.Parent = workspace
    cannonball.Color = Color3.new(0, 0, 0)
    cannonball.Material = Enum.Material.Slate
end
```

Let's run through this step-by-step:

- Line 2: Create a new Part using Instance.new() (you will learn about this in the next chapter.)
- Line 3: Make the cannonball a spherical shape.
- Line 4: Set the cannonball's velocity to go forward and up
  a. Forward: origin.CFrame.lookVector * 300
    1. Shoot toward the front side of origin
  b. Up: Vector3.new(0, 30, 0)
    1. Add a slight up-curve using the y-axis
- Line 5: Set the position of the cannonball to two studs in front of the player's head (to prevent it colliding with the player's head)
- Line 6: Set its size to a 1.5-stud by 1.5-stud by 1.5-stud shape
- Line 7: Set the parent of the cannonball to the workspace, allowing players to view it and interact with it
- Line 8: Change the color of the cannonball to black
- Line 9: Change its material to Slate

Next, for purely visual effects, we can add fire to the cannonball like so:

```lua
    cannonball.Color = Color3.new(0, 0, 0)
    cannonball.Material = Enum.Material.Slate

    local fire = Instance.new("Fire")
    fire.Parent = cannonball
    fire.Size = 4
end
```

And finally, we can detect when the cannonball is touched. If it is, we can create an explosion at that position with this code:

```
    local fire = Instance.new("Fire")
    fire.Parent = cannonball
    fire.Size = 4

    cannonball.Touched:Connect(function(hit)
        local explosion = Instance.new("Explosion")
        explosion.BlastRadius = 20
        explosion.Position = cannonball.Position
        explosion.Parent = workspace
        cannonball:Destroy()
    end)
end
```

This code creates an explosion in the Workspace at the position of the cannonball when it hits something else.

Let's add code to destroy the cannonball after 3 seconds.

```
    cannonball.Touched:Connect(function(hit)
        local explosion = Instance.new("Explosion")
        explosion.BlastRadius = 20
        explosion.Position = cannonball.Position
        explosion.Parent = workspace
        cannonball:Destroy()
    end)

    game.Debris:AddItem(cannonball, 3)
end
```

`game.Debris` is a service that destroys items for you. You can set it to instantly destroy or have it wait. In this case, you destroy the cannonball after waiting 3 seconds.

The finished shoot function should look like this:

```
local function shoot(origin)
    local cannonball = Instance.new("Part")
    cannonball.Shape = Enum.PartType.Ball
    cannonball.Velocity = origin.CFrame.lookVector * 300 + Vector3.new(0, 30, 0)
    cannonball.CFrame = origin.CFrame + Vector3.new(0, 2, 0)
    cannonball.Size = Vector3.new(1.5, 1.5, 1.5)
    cannonball.Parent = workspace
    cannonball.Color = Color3.new(0, 0, 0)
    cannonball.Material = Enum.Material.Slate

    local fire = Instance.new("Fire")
    fire.Parent = cannonball
    fire.Size = 4

    cannonball.Touched:Connect(function(hit)
        local explosion = Instance.new("Explosion")
        explosion.BlastRadius = 20
        explosion.Position = cannonball.Position
        explosion.Parent = workspace
        cannonball:Destroy()
    end)

    game.Debris:AddItem(cannonball, 3)
end
```

Now let's hook this function to the Part being clicked:

```
        local explosion = Instance.new("Explosion")
        explosion.BlastRadius = 20
        explosion.Position = cannonball.Position
        explosion.Parent = workspace
        cannonball:Destroy()
    end)

    game.Debris:AddItem(cannonball, 3)
end

script.Parent.ClickDetector.MouseClick:Connect(function(plr)
    local head = plr.Character.Head
    shoot(head)
end)
```

The (almost) finished code should look like this:

```
local function shoot(origin)
    local cannonball = Instance.new("Part")
    cannonball.Shape = Enum.PartType.Ball
    cannonball.Velocity = origin.CFrame.lookVector * 300 + Vector3.new(0, 30, 0)
    cannonball.CFrame = origin.CFrame + Vector3.new(0, 2, 0)
    cannonball.Size = Vector3.new(1.5, 1.5, 1.5)
    cannonball.Parent = workspace
    cannonball.Color = Color3.new(0, 0, 0)
    cannonball.Material = Enum.Material.Slate

    local fire = Instance.new("Fire")
    fire.Parent = cannonball
    fire.Size = 4

    cannonball.Touched:Connect(function(hit)
        local explosion = Instance.new("Explosion")
        explosion.BlastRadius = 20
        explosion.Position = cannonball.Position
        explosion.Parent = workspace
        cannonball:Destroy()
    end)

    game.Debris:AddItem(cannonball, 3)
end

script.Parent.ClickDetector.MouseClick:Connect(function(plr)
    local head = plr.Character.Head
    shoot(head)
end)
```

You can add a debounce to allow there to be a wait time in between each cannonball shot:

```lua
local debounce = true

local function shoot(origin)
    if debounce then
        debounce = false
        local cannonball = Instance.new("Part")
        cannonball.Shape = Enum.PartType.Ball
        cannonball.Velocity = origin.CFrame.lookVector * 300 + Vector3.new(0, 30, 0)
        cannonball.CFrame = origin.CFrame + Vector3.new(0, 2, 0)
        cannonball.Size = Vector3.new(1.5, 1.5, 1.5)
        cannonball.Parent = workspace
        cannonball.Color = Color3.new(0, 0, 0)
        cannonball.Material = Enum.Material.Slate
        
        local fire = Instance.new("Fire")
        fire.Parent = cannonball
        fire.Size = 4
        
        cannonball.Touched:Connect(function(hit)
            local explosion = Instance.new("Explosion")
            explosion.BlastRadius = 20
            explosion.Position = cannonball.Position
            explosion.Parent = workspace
            cannonball:Destroy()
        end)
        
        game.Debris:AddItem(cannonball, 3)
        
        wait(2)
        debounce = true
    end
end

script.Parent.ClickDetector.MouseClick:Connect(function(plr)
    local head = plr.Character.Head
    shoot(head)
end)
```

Chapter 14. Instances

Instance.new(...)

`Instance.new(...)` is an incredibly useful function. Creating objects is simpler than one could guess. Simply use the `Instance.new()` function and pass the class name of the object that you want to create.

```
local part = Instance.new("Part")
part.Anchored = true
part.BrickColor = BrickColor.new("Really red")
part.Name = "Red Part"
part.Parent = workspace

local msg = Instance.new("Message")
msg.Text = "The name of the part that was created is " .. part.Name
msg.Parent = workspace
```

This is useful for inserting things into the game. For example, suppose you wanted to create several Parts in the workspace. You could manually insert them, or you could create a loop in a Script that uses Instance.new("Part")

```
for i = 1, 10 do
    local newPart = Instance.new("Part")
    newPart.Parent = workspace

    if i % 2 == 0 then
        newPart.BrickColor = BrickColor.new("Really red")
    end

    newPart.Position = Vector3.new(0, i * 2, 0)
    newPart.Anchored = true
end
```

The code above loops ten times. Each time, a new Part is created and placed into the workspace. Every other iteration, this Part is red. Its position is two studs—a stud being a Roblox form of measurement—above the last. A Part's Position is measured using the Vector3 datatype, which is a measurement of something's **x**, **y**, and **z** values.

You can use `Instance.new()` to insert things that you would not normally be able to insert. For example, suppose you wanted to insert a Message into the Workspace.

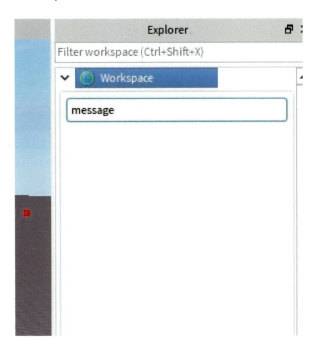

You can insert a message into the workspace (and also set its text) with this code.

```
local message = Instance.new("Message")
message.Parent = workspace
message.Text = "Hello world!"

wait(3)

message:Destroy()
```

The result should be something similar to this.

`Instance.new()` can be used in a variety of ways, such as in a dropper in a tycoon.

Chapter 15. Humanoids

What is a Humanoid?

A Humanoid is a special type of object that allows a Model to function like a character. There are two types of Humanoids: R6 and R15.

R6 Humanoids

1. Have 6 limbs: Head, Torso, Left Arm, Left Leg, Right Arm, Right Leg
2. Head must be attached to Torso, or the Humanoid dies immediately.

R15 Humanoids

1. Have 15 limbs: Head, UpperTorso, LowerTorso, LeftFoot, RightFoot, LeftUpperLeg, RightUpperLeg, LeftUpperArm, RightUpperArm, LeftLowerArm, RightLowerArm, LeftLowerLeg, RightLowerLeg, LeftHand, RightHand
2. Head must be attached to UpperTorso, or Humanoid dies immediately.
3. More complex and robust

One special characteristic of Humanoids is that they allow a Model to have a name. All Humanoids have this basic structure:

In the workspace, that hierarchy looks like this:

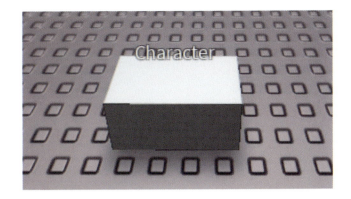

Here is how you can make a basic character:

Step 1. Before we begin, click on the "Join" dropdown at the top of the screen. Select Always. Then, click on the Material caret. Select SmoothPlastic. This causes every Part you insert to be smooth.

Step 2. Insert six parts into the workspace. We will be making an R6 rig (Humanoid character) for now.
- **Tip: Insert one part, select it, copy it (CTRL-C), and paste it (CTRL-V) five times.**

Step 3. Select all of them, and click on the Model tab at the top.

-

Step 4. With all six Parts selected, click Group. You should end up with a Model consisting of the six Parts.

-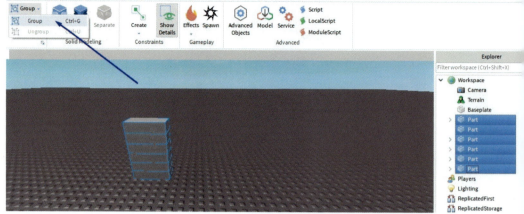
- Step 5. Locate the topmost Part and name it Head. (Either select it in the Explorer and click on it again, or change the Name property through the Properties tab.)
- Step 6. If you don't already have the Toolbox open, click on the View category at the top of the screen and make sure Toolbox is selected.
- Step 7. Go into the Toolbox and click on the dropdown list. From that, select Decals.
- Step 8. Find a face that you like. I will be using this Face Decal:
-
- Step 9. Select the Part you named "Head" in the Explorer. Scroll all the way down in Properties to find "Surface".
- Step 10. Click on the caret (^) next to "Surface" and click on the value of FrontSurface. Select Smooth.

- Step 11. Look back at your Head Part in the workspace. See which side is outlined in a yellow rectangle, and drag your decal (from the Toolbox) onto that side.

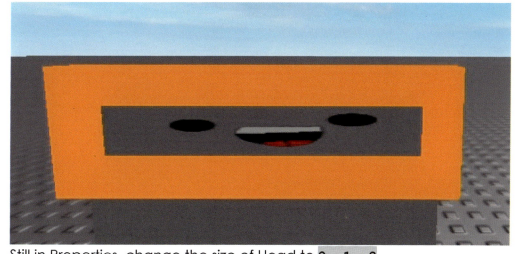

- Step 12. Still in Properties, change the size of Head to **2, 1, 2**
- Step 13. Click on the Model tab at the top. Click on Scale, and bring the green handle up so the Head looks like this: (You are changing the size of the Part.)

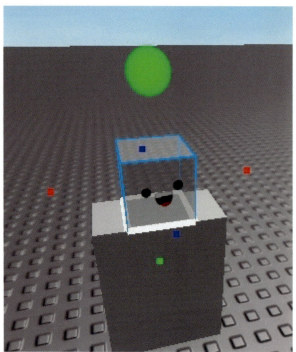

- Step 14. Insert a SpecialMesh into Head. This makes it look like a head.

- Step 15. Select the Part right below the Head. Name it Torso.
- Step 16. Select the Part right below Torso. Name it Left Arm.
- Step 17. Using the Scale button, resize the Left Arm Part to look like this:

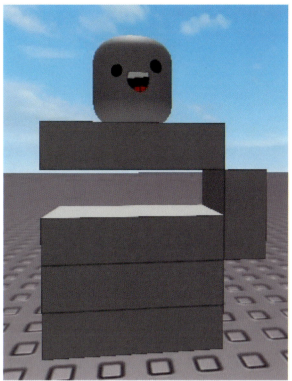

- Step 18. Name the Part below the Torso Right Arm.
- Step 19. Resize the Right Arm so it looks like this:

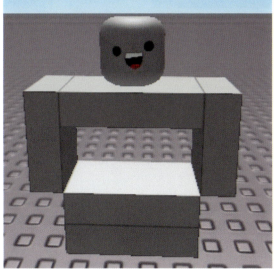

- Step 20. Resize the Torso so it looks like this:

-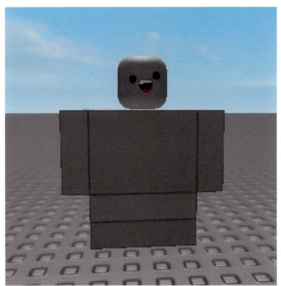
  Step 21. Select the Part right below the Torso. Name it Left Leg.
  Step 22. Select the Part right below Left Leg. Name it Right Leg.
  Step 23. Resize the legs so they look like this (note that the Left Leg should go on the character's left, and same with the right.)
  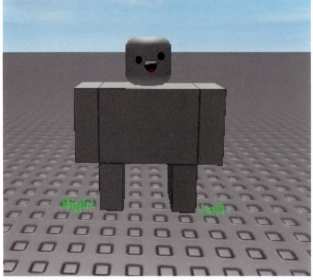
- Step 24. Select the Model tab. Click Move. Select all six Parts in the Explorer, or select the Model.

- Step 25. Click and hold the green arrow. Drag the Model one stud up.
- Step 26. Resize the legs to make them one stud longer.

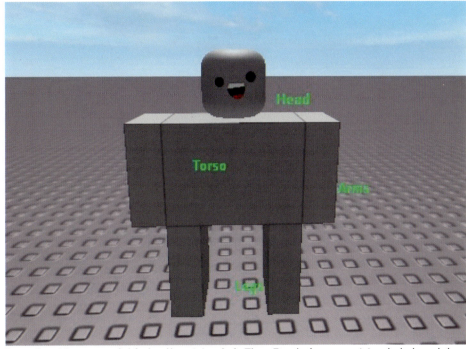

- Step 27. Insert a Humanoid into the Model. The Parts in your Model should now have rounded edges.

-

    Step 28.   Select Humanoid in the Explorer. In the Properties window, change the HealthDisplayType to AlwaysOn.

That's it! You have successfully created a Model with a Humanoid, or an NPC (non-player character.) To test if it works, insert a Part into the workspace, name it FinishPart, and move it somewhere a medium distance from the NPC. Insert a Script into the NPC Model, and add the following code:

```
local humanoid = script.Parent.Humanoid
wait(2)
humanoid:MoveTo(workspace.FinishPart.Position)
```

What does this do?

At line 1, you assign your Humanoid to a variable. At line 2, you wait two seconds. At line 3, you tell the Humanoid to move to the FinishPart. Now click the Play button and test your Humanoid.

Page 70

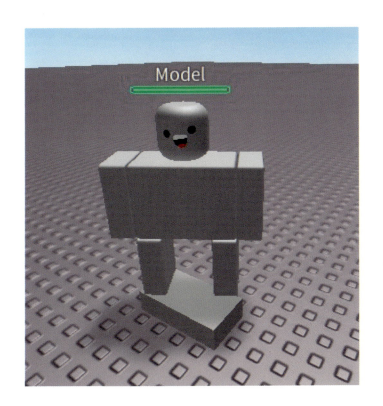

Chapter 16. Values

Variables are good for storing values in Scripts. To have a value be accessible by many Scripts, we can use something called Values.

There are many classes of Values:

1. BoolValue
2. BrickColorValue
3. Color3Value
4. Vector3Value
5. CFrameValue
6. IntValue
7. NumberValue
8. ObjectValue
9. StringValue
10. RayValue

Values are what you would expect. They hold values to certain objects in Roblox. NumberValues hold numbers, StringValues hold strings, BoolValues hold Booleans, and so on. However, they are separated from variables in the fact that values live in the game space, or rather, they are in your Roblox game's DataModel. Hence,

1. BoolValues hold Booleans
2. BrickColorValues hold BrickColors
3. Color3Values hold Color3's
4. Vector3Values hold Vector3's
5. CFrameValues hold CFrame's
6. IntValues hold integers (which are positive and negative whole numbers, as opposed to numbers)
7. NumberValues hold numbers (which are broader than integers, because they can include decimals as well)
8. ObjectValues hold objects (references to objects in your game)
9. StringValues hold strings
10. RayValues hold rays (which you will not learn about in this book)

The DataModel

The DataModel sounds like a complicated programming concept. However, you have used it before. How? When you reference game in your Scripts. The DataModel, also commonly known as game, is the root of your Roblox game's hierarchy. Every object that "exists" in your Roblox game has the DataModel (or game) as its ultimate ancestor.

Values Interacting with Hierarchy

Unlike values, variables live only in your Script environment, values live in the game environment. They are like variables that are accessible by multiple Scripts.

Using values is easy. You simply right-click where you want to insert the value and choose the Value. For example:

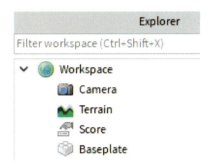

As you can see above, I inserted a NumberValue and named it Score. Notice that in the Properties panel, you can change the Value property. I myself changed this to 250:

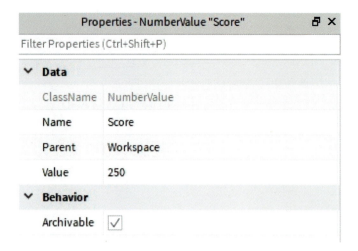

Now insert a Script into the Workspace. Enter the following code:

```
local score = script.Parent.Score
print("Score: " .. score.Value)
```

This isn't very useful at the moment, so let's add a Part that, when touched, increases the score by ten and prints it out.

Start by inserting a Part into the workspace. Delete the Script you have already created and insert a new one into the Part.

Open up the Script you have just inserted. Hook the `Touched` event of its parent Part to a function that increases the score and prints it out (with debounce, of course!) like so:

```
local score = workspace.Score
local debounce = true

script.Parent.Touched:Connect(function()
    if debounce then
        debounce = false

        score.Value = score.Value + 10
        print(score.Value)

        wait(2)
        debounce = true
    end
end)
```

You can even go a step further and use what you learned in Chapter 13 and add a ClickDetector into the Part. You can use this to detect a click instead of a touch and increment and display the score then. You can even use `Instance.new("ClickDetector")` to create the ClickDetector in code.

```
local score = workspace.Score
local debounce = true

local clickDetector = Instance.new("ClickDetector")
clickDetector.Parent = script.Parent

clickDetector.MouseClick:Connect(function()
    if debounce then
        debounce = false

        score.Value = score.Value + 10
        print(score.Value)

        wait(2)
        debounce = true
    end
end)
```

Leaderstats

Values can also be used in leaderboards in Roblox games. Roblox provides a system for leaderboards which you can use in your game. You simply insert an object (I prefer a Folder) into the player object, and then you insert whatever value stats you need into that. Here is an example:

| Player1 | 500 |
| Player | 500 |

Player
Account: <13

That is made from the following code:

```
game.Players.PlayerAdded:Connect(function(plr)
    local leaderstats = Instance.new("Folder")
    leaderstats.Name = "leaderstats"
    leaderstats.Parent = plr

    local score = Instance.new("IntValue")
    score.Name = "Score"
    score.Value = 500
    score.Parent = leaderstats
end)
```

You should be able to tell from this code that whenever a player joins the game, a Folder instance is created and put inside their Player object, and it is named leaderstats. Then, an IntValue (holding an integer) called Score is created and placed into `leaderstats`. Note that the name of the Folder must be `leaderstats`.

Note that you can also use StringValues, NumberValues, and BoolValues. For example:

Page 76

Chapter 17. Guis

In this chapter, you will learn the fundamentals of Scripting with Guis, which are a vital important to most games.

What is a GUI?

A GUI is an acronym for **G**raphical **U**ser **I**nterface, pronounced "gooey". In Roblox, there are three main types of Guis.

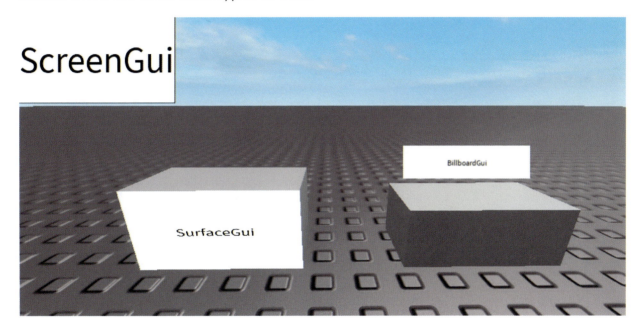

ScreenGuis, SurfaceGuis, and BillboardGuis are only the root of GUI components. To actually display text, you have to insert a Frame into the gui and then a TextLabel into the Frame. Also, most Guis go in the folder of the game called StarterGui:

GUI Sizing and Positioning

Guis use a sizing and positioning system that is different from Part sizing and positioning. While Parts use Vector3 and CFrame, Guis use UDim2. UDim2 is a Roblox object composed of two UDim's. UDim's stand for universal dimension and uses scale and offset. Scale is a number between 0 and 1 that is a percentage of the parent's size. For example, if the scale value was 0.1, then that means the object will take up 10 percent of its parent. If its parent is 100 pixels tall, this means that the object would be 10 pixels tall. Offset is an integer that specifies the precise number of pixels to be measured, as opposed to Scale – which is a percentage. UDim2 instances, which are used in a Gui's size and position, are composed of two UDim2 instances. One determines the x position/size, and the other determines the y position/size. For example:

Size			{0, 100},{0, 100}
⌄ X			0, 100
	Scale		0
	Offset		100
⌄ Y			0, 100
	Scale		0
	Offset		100

A New Type of Script - LocalScript

Before we begin working with Guis, we need to learn about a new type of Scripts – LocalScripts. You need to know that there are several computers that do the work for your game on Roblox. The Roblox game server, which is the computer at Roblox that is hosting your game, does most of the work. All Script objects that you create and write are run by the Roblox game server. However, because the server is away over the network, it can't do everything, or there would be a considerable amount of lag in your Roblox game. Imagine clicking a button only to receive the results several moments later. Imagine seeing your character jump seconds after you pressed the space bar. These are the kinds of things that can happen if all the work is given to the server to handle. LocalScripts are scripts that the client runs. The client is the computer or device that each player is using. All LocalScripts are specific to a player; which player depends on where they are located – for example, in Player1's backpack or character. The player whose client-side computer is running the LocalScript can be accessed with this code:

```
-- A LocalScript inside StarterPlayerScripts in StarterPlayer
local player = game.Players.LocalPlayer
print(player.Name)
```

Using LocalScripts in Guis is not only good practice but also reduces the workload of the server.

Now let's put all this knowledge to the test by creating a ScreenGui and Frame, with the help of a LocalScript:

Insert a LocalScript into StarterGui. In the LocalScript, type this code:

```
local gui = Instance.new("ScreenGui")
gui.Parent = script.Parent

local frame = Instance.new("Frame")
frame.Parent = gui
frame.Size = UDim2.new(1, 0, 0.25, 0)
```

This isn't particularly useful yet. What we can do is add a button into the Frame.

```
local gui = Instance.new("ScreenGui")
gui.Parent = script.Parent

local frame = Instance.new("Frame")
frame.Parent = gui
frame.Size = UDim2.new(1, 0, 0.25, 0)

local button = Instance.new("TextButton")
button.Parent = frame
button.Size = UDim2.new(1, 0, 1, 0)
button.Text = "Click me!"
```

Now we can hook an event that fires whenever the button is clicked:

```
local gui = Instance.new("ScreenGui")
gui.Parent = script.Parent

local frame = Instance.new("Frame")
frame.Parent = gui
frame.Size = UDim2.new(1, 0, 0.25, 0)

local button = Instance.new("TextButton")
button.Parent = frame
button.Size = UDim2.new(1, 0, 1, 0)
button.Text = "Click me!"

local debounce = true
button.MousesButton1Click:Connect(function()
    if debounce then
        debounce = false
        button.Text = "I was clicked!"
        wait(1)
        button.Text = "Click me!!!"
        debounce = true
    end
end)
```

Let's run through what this code does:

At line 1, you assign `gui` to a new ScreenGui. At line 2, you parent the `gui` to the LocalScript's parent, which should be StarterGui. At line 4, you assign `frame` to a new Frame. At line 5, you assign `frame`'s parent to `gui`. At line 6, you set `frame`'s size to occupy 100% of the screen length-wise and 25% of the screen height-wise. At line 8, you assign `button` to a new TextButton. At line 9, you parent the `button` to the `frame`. At line 10, you set the `button`'s size to occupy 100% of the screen length-wise and height-wise. At line 11, you set the `button`'s text to `"Click me!!"` At line 12, you set the `button`'s font size to 40. At line 14, you create a debounce variable. At line 15, you set a listener to the `button`'s click. At line 16, you check to see if `debounce` is triggered or not. At line 17, you set `debounce` to `false`. At line 18, you set the button's text to `"I was clicked!"`. At line 19, you wait one second. At line 20, you change the button's text back to `"Click me!!"` At line 21, you set `debounce` back to `true` to prepare for another click.

Chapter 18. Tycoon

In this chapter, you will be using everything that you learned from this book and creating a tycoon game.

How Do Tycoons Work?

In tycoons, the objective is to gain money from buying items around your base. Buying more droppers and upgraders and upgrading your conveyors will allow you to rake in the cash and finish the tycoon.

Let's get started!

First Things First

Open Roblox Studio. As usual, click Baseplate. Roblox Studio should start up like normal.

Because we are making a basic tycoon, we need a leaderboard to display money, kills, and deaths. In the Toolbox panel, click on the Models dropdown and then click ROBLOX Sets. Under Game Stuff, you should see an item with the text "Leaderboard". Click on that to insert the Script into the workspace. This provides you with a Script called LinkedLeaderboard. We need to edit this Script so that it includes a money value in the leaderboard as well. To do this, we will change the source of the Script to our own script. Click on the Script to view its properties in the Properties panel. Then, open the Script. Copy everything inside the Script (Ctrl-A, Ctrl-C), change the Script's LinkedSource property to [Embedded], and then paste everything back into the Script. Before we move on, hit Ctrl-S to save. Name this "Tycoon". Save it in a memorable place that you can find later.

Now we can add a money value to the player leaderboard. Open the leaderboard Script and scroll down to line 127. You should see this:

```lua
          else

              local stats = Instance.new("IntValue")
              stats.Name = "leaderstats"

              local kills = Instance.new("IntValue")
              kills.Name = "KOs"
              kills.Value = 0

              local deaths = Instance.new("IntValue")
              deaths.Name = "Wipeouts"
              deaths.Value = 0

              kills.Parent = stats
              deaths.Parent = stats

              -- VERY UGLY HACK
              -- Will this leak threads?
              -- Is the problem even what I think it is (player arrived before character)?
              while true do
                  if newPlayer.Character ~= nil then break end
                  wait(5)
              end

              local humanoid = newPlayer.Character.Humanoid

              humanoid.Died:connect(function() onHumanoidDied(humanoid, newPlayer) end )
```

Now we can add a money column to the leaderboard. Type this:

Page 82

```
        else
                local stats = Instance.new("IntValue")
                stats.Name = "leaderstats"

                local kills = Instance.new("IntValue")
                kills.Name = "KOs"
                kills.Value = 0

                local deaths = Instance.new("IntValue")
                deaths.Name = "Wipeouts"
                deaths.Value = 0

                local money = Instance.new("IntValue")
                money.Name = "Money"
                money.Value = 0

                kills.Parent = stats
                deaths.Parent = stats
                money.Parent = stats

                -- VERY UGLY HACK
                -- Will this leak threads?
                -- Is the problem even what I think it is (player arrived before character)?
                while true do
                        if newPlayer.Character ~= nil then break end
                        wait(5)
                end

                local humanoid = newPlayer.Character.Humanoid

                humanoid.Died:connect(function() onHumanoidDied(humanoid, newPlayer) end )

                -- start to listen for new humanoid
                newPlayer.Changed:connect(function(property) onPlayerRespawn(property, newPlayer) end )
```

(Add lines 128-130, and then add line 134 after line 133.

When you play your game, you should see a leaderboard in the top right corner that shows your kills, deaths, and money.

Now we can begin the actual tycoon.

First Steps

Every Tycoon needs a floor! Insert a Part into the workspace. In the Model category at the top of your screen, where it says "1 studs" next to the Move checkbox, change that to .25:

Now resize the floor to however big you want the tycoon to be.

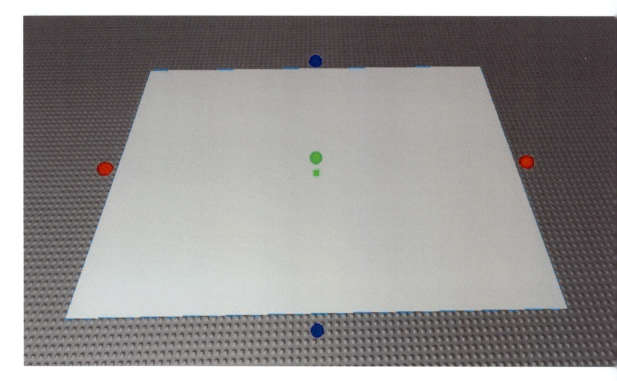

This doesn't really look much like a floor yet. First, name this Part Floor, and then change its material to WoodPlanks and change its color to Wheat:

Appearance	
BrickColor	☐ Wheat
Color	☐ [241, 231, 19...
Material	WoodPlanks
Reflectance	0
Transparency	0

Every tycoon needs a conveyor to transport dropped Parts to be processed. Insert a Part and drag it onto the floor that you created. Then resize it to be about the same height as your floor. Then change its color to Black and its material to SmoothPlastic:

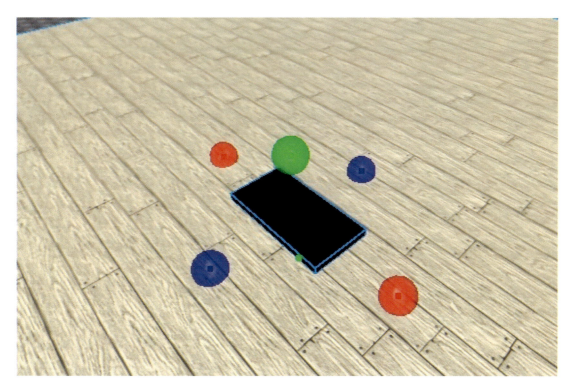

Appearance	
BrickColor	Really black
Color	[17, 17, 17] (...
Material	SmoothPlastic
Reflectance	0

The next step is very important. In the Properties panel, with this Part selected, scroll all the way down until you reach Surface. Click on the caret next to Surface to expand it, and then change FrontSurface to Motor.

BackSurface	Smooth
BottomSurface	Smooth
FrontSurface	Motor
LeftSurface	Smooth
RightSurface	Smooth
TopSurface	Smooth

Now that we know which way the Part is facing (its front surface), we can rotate it accordingly to meet our needs. For example, if the motor on the front surface isn't pointing the way you want it to go, click Rotate at the top of the screen, and then rotate the Part so the motor is facing where you want it to go:

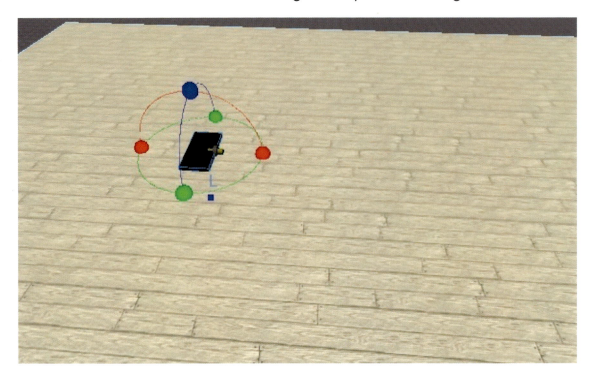

Now you can change the Part's FrontSurface back to Smooth and resize it to however big you want your conveyor to be.

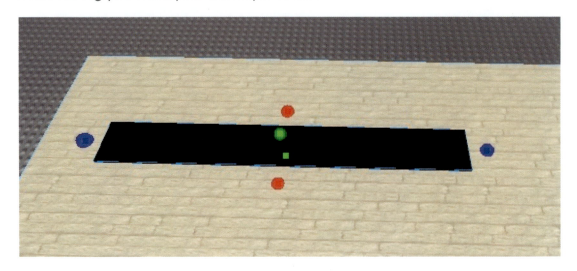

Name this Part Conveyor. Anchor both the conveyor and the floor that you made to make sure that they cannot move around. The conveyor doesn't move yet, so we will add a Script inside the Part. Type this code:

```
while true do
    wait()
    script.Parent.Velocity = script.Parent.CFrame.LookVector * 15
end
```

This means that the Conveyor will move Parts along its surface to its Front Surface. Test it out by playing the game and standing on the conveyor.

Now we can create the basics of a mine. A mine has a button that you click to drop Parts that are worth money. The conveyor will bring the Parts to a place where they are processed and you (or other players) gain the money. For the purpose of this book, we will be using this:

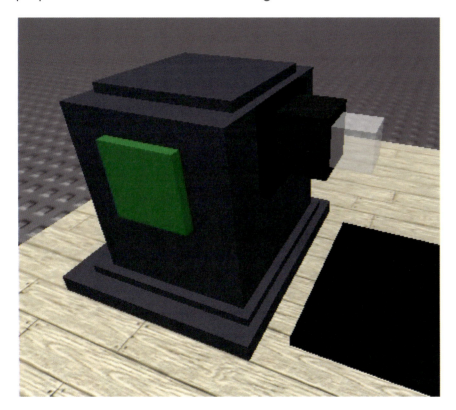

You can find this mine at the link:
https://www.roblox.com/library/2108904696/Tycoon-Mine. You can grab one and then go into Roblox Studio and in the Toolbox, click on the dropdown and click on My Models. You should see the mine there.

Once you have created a mine, add a Part and name it DropPart. Position it using the Move button (at the top of your screen) to where you want Parts to come out of your mine. Then view DropPart in the Properties panel. Uncheck the CanCollide checkbox, so Parts will be able to go through it. Also make sure that the button's BrickColor is Lime green. Now select every Part in the mine and press Ctrl-G to group the Parts into a Model. If you made a mistake, use Ctrl-Z to undo. Name the Model Mine. Now insert a Configuration Folder into the mine and name it Config:

We will be adding two values in this folder – an IntValue representing how much each dropped Part is worth, and an NumberValue showing how much time to wait in between button clicks. Insert an IntValue into the configuration folder and change its Value in the Properties panel to 1. Insert a NumberValue into the configuration folder and change its name to Cooldown, and set its value to 0.1. You will see that it shows up as 0.10000000000000000555, but that's okay. It's a very close approximation of the number, since you can't get precisely 0.1 with computers. This is because computers process decimals as binary fractions added to one another. So, for example, 0.5 = ½, 0.75 = ½ + ¼, and 0.375 = ¼ + ⅛. There is no way to get 0.1 using this method without running out of bits, so the computer uses the closest value it can. When you print the value using the command bar, the output will show 0.1:

```
> print(workspace.Mine.Config.Cooldown.Value)
0.1
```

Now that we have set up proper configurations for the Mine, we can add a Script to it to make it work. Before we make the mine work, we need to insert a Folder into the workspace that contains all of our parts that have been dropped (for organization purposes).

Now we can insert a Script into the button, and hook up the ClickDetector inside the button Part (make sure you have one) to flash the button red and insert a new Part like so:

```lua
local button = script.Parent
local config = button.Parent.Config
local debounce = true

button.ClickDetector.MouseClick:Connect(function()
    if debounce then
        debounce = false
        button.BrickColor = BrickColor.Red()

        local part = Instance.new("Part")
        part.Size = Vector3.new(1, 1, 1)
        part.CFrame = button.Parent.DropPart.CFrame
        part.Material = Enum.Material.SmoothPlastic
        part.Name = "Drop"

        game.Debris:AddItem(part, 120)
        part.Parent = workspace.DroppedParts

        wait(config.Cooldown.Value)
        button.BrickColor = BrickColor.new("Lime green")
        debounce = true
    end
end)
```

You may have noticed that while we use Cooldown from the configuration folder, we don't use Value. Let's change that.

```
local button = script.Parent
local config = button.Parent.Config
local debounce = true

button.ClickDetector.MouseClick:Connect(function()
    if debounce then
        debounce = false
        button.BrickColor = BrickColor.Red()

        local part = Instance.new("Part")
        part.Size = Vector3.new(1, 1, 1)
        part.CFrame = button.Parent.DropPart.CFrame
        part.Material = Enum.Material.SmoothPlastic
        part.Name = "Drop"

        local value = config.Value:Clone()
        value.Parent = part

        game.Debris:AddItem(part, 120)
        part.Parent = workspace.DroppedParts

        wait(config.Cooldown.Value)
        button.BrickColor = BrickColor.new("Lime green")
        debounce = true
    end
end)
```

This Script can be shortened even further:

```
local button = script.Parent
local config = button.Parent.Config
local debounce = true

button.ClickDetector.MouseClick:Connect(function()
    if debounce then
        debounce = false
        button.BrickColor = BrickColor.Red()

        local part = Instance.new("Part")
        part.Size = Vector3.new(1, 1, 1)
        part.CFrame = button.Parent.DropPart.CFrame
        part.Material = Enum.Material.SmoothPlastic
        part.Name = "Drop"

        config.Value:Clone().Parent = part

        game.Debris:AddItem(part, 120)
        part.Parent = workspace.DroppedParts

        wait(config.Cooldown.Value)
        button.BrickColor = BrickColor.new("Lime green")
        debounce = true
    end
end)
```

A line-by-line explanation of this Script:

At line 1, you assign the `button` variable to the script's parent. At line 2, you assign `config` to the configuration folder that you created. At line 3, you create a `debounce` variable. At line 5, you add a listener to button clicks. At line 6, you check the `debounce` variable to see if you are able to click the `button` and drop a new Part. At line 7, you set the `debounce` value to `false` to prevent further clicks. At line 8, you set the button's color to red to show that the button can't be clicked for the time being. At line 10, we create a new Part. From lines 11-14, you set the size of the Part to 1 by 1 by 1 stud, set its position to the DropPart's position, make all of its surfaces smooth, and name it Drop. At line 16, you clone the value (denoting how much the drop is worth) and put it into the Part. At line 18, you add the Part to `game.Debris` to cause it to expire in 120 seconds. At line 19, you parent the Part to DroppedParts for organization purposes. At line 21, you tell the Script to wait the cooldown time. At line 22, you change the button's color back to green, and at line 23, you allow the button to be clickable again.

Great! Now, we still need buttons, money, a cash collector, cash giver, and a gate. We can amend that right now!

Adding a Gate

The gate to claim ownership of the tycoon is the most important thing required right now. You can build a simple gate with two cylinders and a Part in the middle that looks like this:

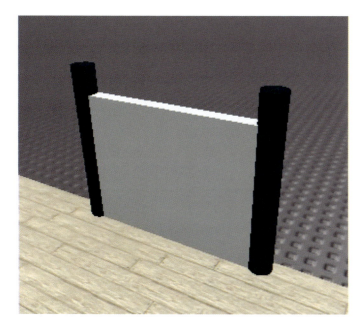

Or you can get the Model from this link:

https://www.roblox.com/library/2111587022/Tycoon-Gate

Place the gate where you want people to claim ownership of the tycoon. Now we can begin Scripting the gate. However, before we do that, we can add a BillboardGui to display text above the gate.

Insert a BillboardGui into the Part of the gate where you want people to enter. This Part should be called Entry. Set AlwaysOnTop to true so that you will be able to see it above every other Part. Set the SizeOffset to 3.5 so you can see it above the gate. Then change the LightInfluence to 0 so its color doesn't change with the lighting. Also change its MaxDistance to 80 so that you can't see it if you are more than 80 studs away. Set Size to {10, 0}, {3, 0} to make the gui 10 studs wide and 3 studs tall (relative to how close the camera is to the gui). Insert a TextLabel into the gui, since you can use a TextLabel in guis without Frames. Change its size to {1, 0}, {1, 0} and its text to Vacant tycoon (or some other text denoting that the tycoon can be claimed). Also check the TextScaled checkbox, which changes the size of the text based on the position of the camera. Now we can begin scripting the gate.

Insert a script into the gate Model. Type the code:

```
local entry = script.Parent.EntryPart
local owner = script.Parent.Parent.Parent.Owner

entry.Touched:Connect(function(hit)
    local plr = game.Players:GetPlayerFromCharacter(hit.Parent)
    if plr then
    
    end
end)
```

Lines 1, 2, 4, 6, and 7 you will understand. However, line 3 may be confusing. Let's rewind to see what `hit` is. `hit`, the parameter to the anonymous function that you create, represents the Part that touched `entry`. If `hit.Parent` is a player's character model, then you can use that to get a player from that character model. At line 4, you check if it exists. If it does, the Script moves on to line 5.

Now we can set a marker to show that a player already owns a tycoon.

```
local entry = script.Parent.EntryPart
local owner = script.Parent.Parent.Parent.Owner

entry.Touched:Connect(function(hit)
    local plr = game.Players:GetPlayerFromCharacter(hit.Parent)
    if plr then
        if not plr:FindFirstChild("OwnsTycoon") then
            local glue = Instance.new("Glue")
            glue.Name = "OwnsTycoon"
            glue.Parent = plr

            wait(0.1)
            entry.CanCollide = false
            entry.Transparency = 0.3
            entry.BillboardGui.TextLabel.Text = plr.Name .. "'s Tycoon"
        end
    end
end)
```

Line 6 creates an Instance of Glue. Line 7 sets the name of the Glue to "OwnsTycoon". Line 8 sets the Glue's Parent to the player that claimed the tycoon. Here I use Glue because it "sticks" with the player. Line 10 forces the Script to wait a tenth of a second. Line 11 enables players to walk through `entry`. Line 12 sets the visibility of `entry` to about 70% visible, and line 13 changes the Text of "Vacant tycoon" to "(player's name)'s Tycoon"

This Script will not work correctly if there are multiple players that do not have a tycoon and try to claim it. For example, consider 4 players. Player1 already has a tycoon and so is not able to claim another. Player2, Player3, and Player4 do not have tycoons. Player2 tries to claim the tycoon, and the text changes to "Player2's Tycoon". Player3 then tries to claim the tycoon. Because Player3 has not already claimed a tycoon, they are allowed to claim Player2's tycoon. There is no check to see if the tycoon already has an owner, so we need to fix that.

Insert an ObjectValue into the Workspace, and name it Owner. Now would be a good time to group all the things that you have created into one tycoon model. Select DroppedParts, Owner, Gate, Mine, Conveyor, and Floor (using Ctrl-Click) and press Ctrl-G to group them into a Model. Name this Model Tycoon #1. (You can change this later on.)

Now we can finish up the gate Script.

```lua
local entry = script.Parent.EntryPart
local owner = script.Parent.Parent.Parent.Owner

entry.Touched:Connect(function(hit)
    local plr = game.Players:GetPlayerFromCharacter(hit.Parent)
    if plr then
        if not plr:FindFirstChild("OwnsTycoon") then
            if not owner.Value then
                local glue = Instance.new("Glue")
                glue.Name = "OwnsTycoon"
                glue.Parent = plr
                
                wait(0.1)
                entry.CanCollide = false
                entry.Transparency = 0.3
                entry.BillboardGui.TextLabel.Text = plr.Name .. "'s Tycoon"
                owner.Value = plr
            end
        end
    end
end)
```

Notice the additions at lines 8 and 17. Line 8 checks if the tycoon has an owner yet, and line 17 sets the Owner value to the first player that claims the tycoon.

Now we can begin to work on the most essential part of Tycoons – the buttons.

The Buttons

To create a Button, we need a button Model. You can create one by inserting a Cylinder in the Home or Model tabs at the top of your screen. You can click on the dropdown under Part, and then select Cylinder. Then, you can rotate it using the Rotate button under the Home or Model tabs at the top of your screen, so that it faces up. You can then resize it and recolor it to look like this:

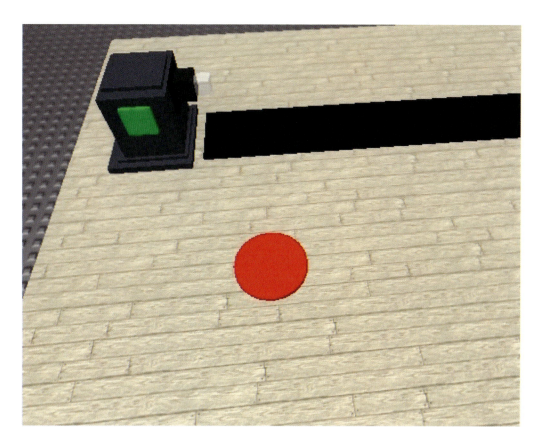

We can create a Folder to organize Buttons and Purchases. Insert three Folders into the tycoon model (Tycoon #1). Name them Buttons, Purchases, and Essentials. Now drag the Conveyor, Floor, and Gate into the Essentials folder.

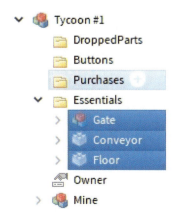

Select the button that you created and name it Head. We will need a few Values for your button as configurations, as well as a BillboardGui (like the one in the gate) to display the object to buy as well as the price required to buy it.

Insert an IntValue, StringValue, BoolValue and BillboardGui into the Script. The IntValue will be named Price; the StringValue will be the name of the object to buy (from the Purchases folder); the BoolValue will represent if the button is being used to buy or upgrade something; and the BillboardGui will display all of these.

Because this will be the first button that players purchase in your tycoon (to get the ball rolling and allow them to make more money to buy other buttons), the price of this button will be free. Name the IntValue Price. Name the StringValue Object. Name the BoolValue IsUpgrade.

Now we can edit the properties of the BillboardGui. Again, check AlwaysOnTop, set SizeOffset to 2 and set LightInfluence to 0. Also set Size to {7, 0}, {1.5, 0}.

Now insert a TextLabel into the BillboardGui. Again, set TextScaled to true and set Size to {1, 0,}, {1, 0}. Make the Text of the TextLabel blank. Uncheck the Visible checkbox. You will see why in a moment. The StringValue needs to be edited to refer to the Mine to buy. Open up the Object StringValue in the Properties panel. Click on Value and change the text to "Mine" (without the quotes).

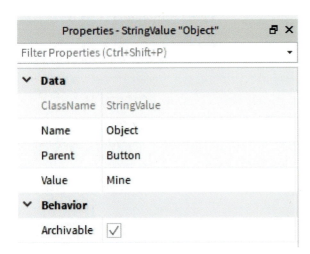

Now drag the Part that you made for the Button into the Buttons folder.

Buttons don't work without a Script, however. Insert a Script into the tycoon Model (Tycoon #1) and name it CoreScript. Before we edit this, however, the gate and Mine Scripts need to be changed. Open the Mine Script first. Change

Page 96

`workspace.DroppedParts` to `script.Parent.Parent.Parent.Parent.DroppedParts`.

```
local button = script.Parent
local config = button.Parent.Config
local debounce = true

button.ClickDetector.MouseClick:Connect(function()
    if debounce then
        debounce = false
        button.BrickColor = BrickColor.Red()

        local part = Instance.new("Part")
        part.Size = Vector3.new(1, 1, 1)
        part.CFrame = button.Parent.DropPart.CFrame
        part.Material = Enum.Material.SmoothPlastic
        part.Name = "Drop"

        config.Value:Clone().Parent = part

        game.Debris:AddItem(part, 120)
        part.Parent = script.Parent.Parent.Parent.Parent.DroppedParts

        wait(config.Cooldown.Value)
        button.BrickColor = BrickColor.new("Lime green")
        debounce = true
    end
end)
```

Now move the Mine into the Purchases folder. Open up the Gate Script and change `script.Parent.Parent.Owner` to `script.Parent.Parent.Parent.Owner`.

```
local entry = script.Parent.EntryPart
local owner = script.Parent.Parent.Parent.Owner

entry.Touched:Connect(function(hit)
    local plr = game.Players:GetPlayerFromCharacter(hit.Parent)
    if plr then
        if not plr:FindFirstChild("OwnsTycoon") then
            if not owner.Value then
                local glue = Instance.new("Glue")
                glue.Name = "OwnsTycoon"
                glue.Parent = plr

                wait(0.1)
                entry.CanCollide = false
                entry.Transparency = 0.3
                entry.BillboardGui.TextLabel.Text = plr.Name .. "'s Tycoon"
                owner.Value = plr
            end
        end
    end
end)
```

You can't buy buttons without money. Insert a Folder into ServerStorage, so the money will be stored on the server, so clients will not be able to hack and change it. Name the Folder PlayerMoney. This will be a container for the money of the players that join your game. Insert a Script into ServerScriptService. This Script will have a listener for whenever a player joins the game, inserting a value into PlayerMoney in ServerStorage. It will also have a listener to change the leaderboard value whenever the value in ServerStorage is changed. Furthermore, when players are leaving, this value will be destroyed.

```lua
game.Players.PlayerAdded:Connect(function(plr)
    local value = Instance.new("IntValue")
    value.Name = plr.Name
    value.Parent = game.ServerStorage.PlayerMoney

    value.Changed:Connect(function(money)
        plr:WaitForChild("leaderstats").Money.Value = money
    end)
end)
game.Players.PlayerRemoving:Connect(function(plr)
    local value = game.ServerStorage.PlayerMoney:WaitForChild(plr.Name)
    value:Destroy()
end)
```

Now we can add a collector Part in front of the conveyor. Whenever parts dropped by the mine touch this Part, they are destroyed, and the cash value is added to the owner's cash to collect value – which we need to create a Part for.

Insert a Part into the Workspace and name it Collector. Drag it to the end of the conveyor and resize it to how big you want your collector to be.

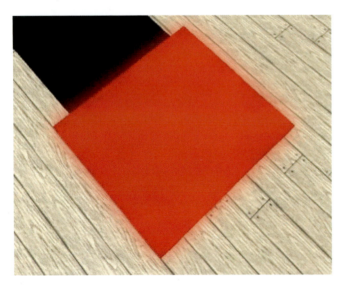

Now insert a Script into the Part. We need to make it so that every time a Part touches the collector Part, the Script checks to see if there is an IntValue in it called Value. If there is, add it to the owner's money.

```
script.Parent.Touched:Connect(function(hit)
    local value = hit:FindFirstChild("Value")
    if value then
        local owner = script.Parent.Parent.Parent.Owner.Value
        if owner then
            local ownerCash = game.ServerStorage.PlayerMoney:FindFirstChild(owner.Name)
            ownerCash.Value = ownerCash.Value + value.Value
        end

        game.Debris:AddItem(hit, 0.1)
    end
end)
```

We need to check at line 3 if the Part that touched the collector has a Value IntValue in it. If it does, the Script gets the Owner value of the tycoon. Then, if there is an owner, the Script increments the owner's money by the value of the Part that touched the collector. Then, the Part is destroyed.

Creating a giver

If you want there to be a button that players walk over to collect money, insert a Part into the Workspace and resize it to however large your button should be. Then name this Part CashCollect. Now add another Part into the Workspace. This Part will display how much money the owner has to collect. Name this Part Head. Now press Ctrl-G to group the Head Part and make it a Model. Add a Humanoid into the Model and change Health and MaxHealth to 0. Select the Model and group it again (Ctrl-G). Now move all other Parts that are part of the giver except the Part named Head into the outer Model. Also name the outer Model Giver:

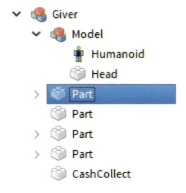

The giver Model will be available at

https://www.roblox.com/library/2149464123/Tycoon-Giver

Insert an IntValue into the tycoon named CashToCollect. Now drag the giver Model into the Essentials folder of the tycoon. Insert a Script to begin coding the giver.

```lua
local tycoon = script.Parent.Parent.Parent
local cashToCollect = tycoon.CashToCollect
local debounce = true

cashToCollect.Changed:Connect(function(cash)
    script.Parent:FindFirstChildOfClass("Model").Name = "Cash to collect: $" .. cash
end)

script.Parent.CashCollect.Touched:Connect(function(hit)
    local plr = game.Players:GetPlayerFromCharacter(hit.Parent)
    if plr then
        if plr == tycoon.Owner.Value then
            if hit.Parent:FindFirstChild("Humanoid") then
                if hit.Parent.Humanoid.Health > 0 then
                    if debounce then
                        debounce = false
                        script.Parent.CashCollect.BrickColor = BrickColor.new("Really red")

                        local plrMoney = game.ServerStorage.PlayerMoney[plr.Name]
                        plrMoney.Value = plrMoney.Value + cashToCollect.Value
                        cashToCollect.Value = 0

                        wait(1)
                        script.Parent.CashCollect.BrickColor = BrickColor.new("Lime green")
                        debounce = true
                    end
                end
            end
        end
    end
end)
```

At this point, you should understand what each of these lines does. Lines 1-3 are relatively simple to comprehend. Lines 5-7 hook a listener to whenever the CashToCollect IntValue is changed. When fired, this listener finds the Model with a Humanoid and changes its name to the proper text to display.

Lines 9-31 hook a listener to the when the CashCollect Part is touched. Line 10 finds the player (if there is one) that touched the Part using the player's character Model. Line 11 checks if a player exists, line 12 checks if the player is the tycoon's owner, lines 13 and 14 check if the player is alive, and line 15 checks if the **debounce** is set to true – meaning that the player is able to collect the cash again. If all of these conditions are true, then **debounce** is set to false, and the color of the CashCollect button Part is set to Really red. The player's money is incremented by the CashToCollect value, and the CashToCollect IntValue is set to 0. The Script waits 1 second, sets the BrickColor of the button back to green again, and sets **debounce** to true.

Now we need to edit the Collector Script so that instead of sending money to the player's ServerStorage value, the money is sent to the CashToCollect value in the tycoon.

Open the Script in the Collector Part. Select these lines:

```
1  script.Parent.Touched:Connect(function(hit)
2      local value = hit:FindFirstChild("Value")
3      if value then
4          local owner = script.Parent.Parent.Parent.Owner.Value
5          if owner then
6              local ownerCash =
7                   game.ServerStorage.PlayerMoney:FindFirstChild(owner.Name)
8
9              ownerCash.Value = ownerCash.Value + value.Value
10         end
11
12         game.Debris:AddItem(hit, 0.1)
13     end
14 end)
```

Now press Backspace (or Delete) and replace it with the following:

```
script.Parent.Touched:Connect(function(hit)
    local value = hit:FindFirstChild("Value")
    if value then
        local owner = script.Parent.Parent.Parent.Owner.Value
        if owner then
            local toCollect = script.Parent.Parent.Parent.CashToCollect
            toCollect.Value = toCollect.Value + value.Value
        end

        game.Debris:AddItem(hit, 0.1)
    end
end)
```

Test the game. If the code is correct, everything should work. Touch the gate to claim the tycoon, and click on the button on the Mine to add to the CashToCollect value. Then walk over the giver to collect the money and view the leaderboard to see the changes.

Coding the button(s)

The Mine shouldn't be visible until the owner buys it. We can fix this by writing the CoreScript. Open the CoreScript inside the tycoon and type the code:

```
local objects = {}
local guis = {}
local buttons = script.Parent:WaitForChild("Buttons")
local purchases = script.Parent:WaitForChild("Purchases")

for i,v in pairs(buttons:GetChildren()) do

end
```

You should understand what these lines mean, if not their purpose. Line 1 creates a table of objects to store the objects of the buttons for later. Why? When you enter a tycoon, you are expected to buy the objects. They shouldn't be visible (or usable) before you buy them. You need the Buttons in order to loop through them, get their objects (from Purchases), and destroy them.

```
local objects = {}
local guis = {}
local buttons = script.Parent:WaitForChild("Buttons")
local purchases = script.Parent:WaitForChild("Purchases")

for i,v in pairs(buttons:GetChildren()) do
    local obj = purchases:WaitForChild(v.Object.Value)
    objects[obj.Name] = obj:Clone()
    obj:Destroy()
end
```

If you run the game now, you should see that the Mine is invisible. Now we can edit the text of the TextLabel to display buying or upgrading the object.

```
local objects = {}
local guis = {}
local buttons = script.Parent:WaitForChild("Buttons")
local purchases = script.Parent:WaitForChild("Purchases")

for i,v in pairs(buttons:GetChildren()) do
    local obj = purchases:WaitForChild(v.Object.Value)
    objects[obj.Name] = obj:Clone()
    obj:Destroy()
    
    local txt = v.BillboardGui.TextLabel
    if v.IsUpgrade.Value then
        txt.Text = "Upgrade to "
    else
        txt.Text = "Buy "
    end
    
    txt.Text = txt.Text .. obj.Name .. ": $" .. v.Price.Value
    guis[#guis] = v.BillboardGui
end
```

Notice that you cannot see the button's text even if you own the tycoon. We will amend that. What we will do is move the BillboardGui into the owner's PlayerGui and set the Adornee of the BillboardGui to the button. You will see why and what this does in a moment.

```lua
local objects = {}
local guis = {}
local buttons = script.Parent:WaitForChild("Buttons")
local purchases = script.Parent:WaitForChild("Purchases")

for i,v in pairs(buttons:GetChildren()) do
    local obj = purchases:WaitForChild(v.Object.Value)
    objects[obj.Name] = obj:Clone()
    obj:Destroy()
    
    local txt = v.BillboardGui.TextLabel
    if v.IsUpgrade.Value then
        txt.Text = "Upgrade to "
    else
        txt.Text = "Buy "
    end
    
    txt.Text = txt.Text .. obj.Name .. ": $" .. v.Price.Value
    guis[#guis] = v.BillboardGui
end

while script.Parent.Owner.Value == nil do wait() end

for i,v in pairs(guis) do
    v.Adornee = v.Parent
    v.Parent = script.Parent.Owner.Value.PlayerGui
end
```

Everything added does this:

1. Sets the Parent of each BillboardGui to the owner's PlayerGui.
2. Sets the Adornee of each BillboardGui to their respective buttons.

The purpose of this is to make the Guis over each button visible only to the owner. First, the guis are stored into a table named `guis`. Then, the Script waits until a player claims the tycoon. After that, each gui's Parent is set to the owner's PlayerGui, and their Adornee is set to the buttons that they used to be under. What this means is that the BillboardGuis will be above the buttons that they represent:

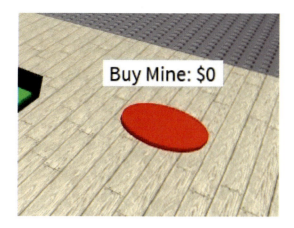

Buying the Object

Now comes the fun (and easy) part – making the button *work!* First, however, we need to insert a Folder into the tycoon named PurchasedObjects.

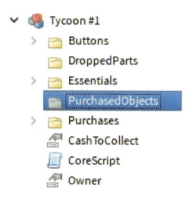

Now we can edit the CoreScript again. We will begin by adding a **Touched** event to the loop.

```
local txt = v.BillboardGui.TextLabel

if v.IsUpgrade.Value then
    txt.Text = "Upgrade to "
else
    txt.Text = "Buy "
end

txt.Text = txt.Text .. obj.Name .. ": $" .. v.Price.Value
guis[#guis] = v.BillboardGui

v.Touched:Connect(function(hit)

end)
```

Page 105

This is for when the owner of the tycoon walks over the button. Now we need to perform several checks to see if the owner can buy the button.

```
txt.Text = txt.Text .. obj.Name .. ": $" .. v.Price.Value
guis[#guis] = v.BillboardGui

v.Touched:Connect(function(hit)
    local char = hit.Parent
    local plr = game.Players:GetPlayerFromCharacter(char)
    if plr then
        if plr == script.Parent.Owner.Value then
            
        end
    end
end)
```

These lines check

1. Whether a player touched the button
2. Whether the player is the owner

```
txt.Text = txt.Text .. obj.Name .. ": $" .. v.Price.Value
guis[#guis] = v.BillboardGui

v.Touched:Connect(function(hit)
    local char = hit.Parent
    local plr = game.Players:GetPlayerFromCharacter(char)
    if plr then
        if plr == script.Parent.Owner.Value then
            local hum = char:FindFirstChild("Humanoid")
            if hum then
                if hum.Health > 0 then
                    
                end
            end
        end
    end
end)
```

The added if-statements check if the player is alive – checking if there is a Humanoid, and if there is, if its health is greater than 0.

Now comes the fun stuff – adding the code to make the button disappear and the object to purchase appear. Before we do so, we need to think about how we will do that. Luckily, we can use the objects table to solve this problem.

```lua
v.Touched:Connect(function(hit)
    local char = hit.Parent
    local plr = game.Players:GetPlayerFromCharacter(char)
    if plr then
        if plr == script.Parent.Owner.Value then
            local hum = char:FindFirstChild("Humanoid")
            if hum then
                if hum.Health > 0 then
                    local plrMoney = game.ServerStorage.PlayerMoney:FindFirstChild(plr.Name)
                    if plrMoney.Value > v.Price.Value then
                        objects[obj.Name].Parent = script.Parent.PurchasedObjects
                        plrMoney.Value = plrMoney.Value - v.Price.Value
                    end
                end
            end
        end
    end
end)
```

The added code checks if the player's cash value is greater than the price required to buy the button. Then, the clone of the object is put inside the PurchasedObjects Folder, and the player's money is subtracted by the price of the button.

There is a problem, however. The button stays where it is even after it is purchased. We can create a nice fade-out effect for the button.

```lua
v.Touched:Connect(function(hit)
    local char = hit.Parent
    local plr = game.Players:GetPlayerFromCharacter(char)
    if plr then
        if plr == script.Parent.Owner.Value then
            local hum = char:FindFirstChild("Humanoid")
            if hum then
                if hum.Health > 0 then
                    local plrMoney = game.ServerStorage.PlayerMoney:FindFirstChild(plr.Name)
                    if plrMoney.Value >= v.Price.Value then
                        objects[obj.Name].Parent = script.Parent.PurchasedObjects
                        plrMoney.Value = plrMoney.Value - v.Price.Value
                        
                        for i = 1, 20 do
                            v.Transparency = v.Transparency + 0.05
                            txt.BackgroundTransparency = txt.BackgroundTransparency + 0.05
                            txt.TextTransparency = txt.TextTransparency + 0.05
                            
                            wait(0.05)
                        end
                        
                        v:Destroy()
                    end
                end
            end
        end
    end
end)
```

The code above adds a gradual fade-out effect for the button and the gui, and then eventually destroys them.

The full code of the CoreScript should look like this:

```lua
local objects = {}
local guis = {}
local buttons = script.Parent:WaitForChild("Buttons")
local purchases = script.Parent:WaitForChild("Purchases")

for i,v in pairs(buttons:GetChildren()) do
    local obj = purchases:WaitForChild(v.Object.Value)
    objects[obj.Name] = obj:Clone()
    obj:Destroy()

    local txt = v.BillboardGui.TextLabel
    if v.IsUpgrade.Value then
        txt.Text = "Upgrade to "
    else
        txt.Text = "Buy "
    end

    txt.Text = txt.Text .. obj.Name .. ": $" .. v.Price.Value
    guis[#guis] = v.BillboardGui

    v.Touched:Connect(function(hit)
        local char = hit.Parent
        local plr = game.Players:GetPlayerFromCharacter(char)
        if plr then
            if plr == script.Parent.Owner.Value then
                local hum = char:FindFirstChild("Humanoid")
                if hum then
                    if hum.Health > 0 then
                        local plrMoney = game.ServerStorage.PlayerMoney:FindFirstChild(plr.Name)
                        if plrMoney.Value >= v.Price.Value then
                            objects[obj.Name].Parent = script.Parent.PurchasedObjects
                            plrMoney.Value = plrMoney.Value - v.Price.Value

                            for i = 1, 20 do
                                v.Transparency = v.Transparency + 0.05
                                txt.BackgroundTransparency = txt.BackgroundTransparency + 0.05
                                txt.TextTransparency = txt.TextTransparency + 0.05

                                wait(0.05)
                            end

                            v:Destroy()
                        end
                    end
                end
            end
        end
    end)
end

while script.Parent.Owner.Value == nil do wait() end

for i,v in pairs(guis) do
    v.Adornee = v.Parent
    v.Parent = script.Parent.Owner.Value.PlayerGui
end
```

Voila! Give yourself a pat on the back for all this code. If you typed everything out correctly, this should work. If it doesn't, look in the Output log and see which Script the error occurred in. Go back to that Script, and compare it to what is shown in this book. With that, you should have a successful tycoon!

More Buttons!

Congratulations! You have created a tycoon. However, no tycoon's a tycoon without multiple buttons. And adding another is quite simple. How? First, select the button that you created in the Explorer panel.

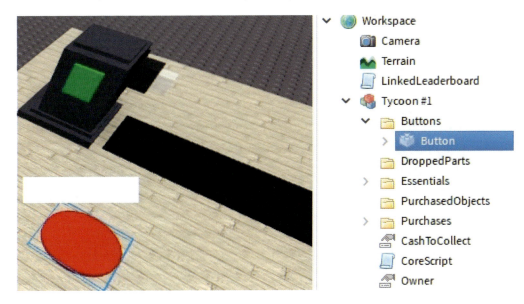

In the Home category at the top of the screen, make sure Collisions is off. Now press Ctrl-D to duplicate.

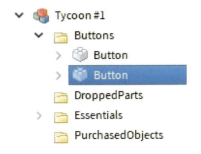

Use the Move button at the top of the screen to move the button where you want the next button to be.

Page 109

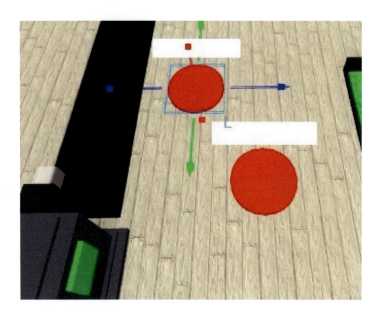

The second purchase in the tycoon will be a dropper. The Model will be available at this link:

https://www.roblox.com/library/2102831636/Basic-Tycoon-Dropper

First things first – make sure that the Model has a Part where you want the dropped Part to come out of. Name this Part DropPart. Then move the Model into the tycoon's Purchases Folder. Also make sure that the Model is named Dropper1. Now set the Object StringValue to Dropper1. Change the Price value to 20, too. The player should have to gain $20 before being allowed to purchase the dropper. If you run your tycoon now, everything *should* work.

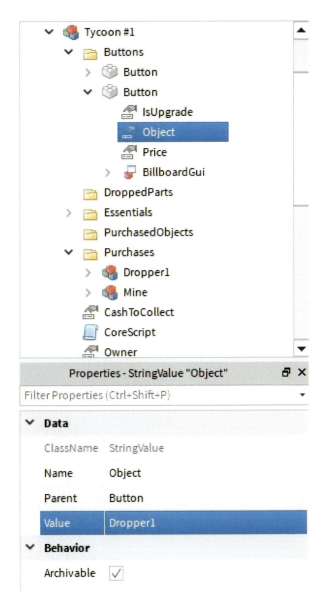

Insert a Script into the dropper. This Script will control the Part-dropping mechanic of the dropper. Also, like the Mine, insert a Configuration folder into the dropper, and name it Config. Insert a NumberValue and IntValue into this folder. Name the NumberValue Cooldown, and leave the IntValue's Name as Value. Open the Script that you inserted.

```
local config = script.Parent.Config

while wait(config.Cooldown.Value) do
    local part = Instance.new("Part")
    part.Size = Vector3.new(1, 1, 1)
    part.CFrame = script.Parent.DropPart.CFrame
    part.Material = Enum.Material.SmoothPlastic
    part.Name = "Drop"
    
    config.Value:Clone().Parent = part
    
    game.Debris:AddItem(part, 120)
    part.Parent = script.Parent.Parent.Parent.DroppedParts
end
```

This code is essentially the same as the code for the Mine except it waits an interval instead of a cooldown, and drops a Part after the interval – as opposed to waiting for a button click.

Change Cooldown's Value to 1, because having a Part drop every 0.1 seconds is too fast. Also change Value's Value to 5.

Another Dropper

We can add another dropper relatively easily. Select the button for the Dropper and press Ctrl-D to duplicate. Move the button a few studs over to where you want the button for the next dropper to be.

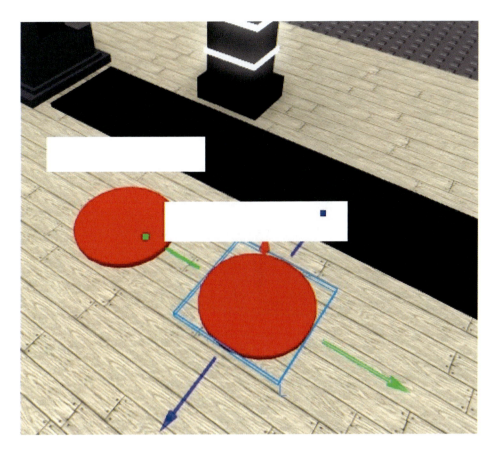

Inside the button, mess around with the values. I think that this button should cost $35, not be an upgrade, and be for a Dropper2. So, change the Price to 35 and Object to Dropper2 instead of Dropper1.

Because all the Scripts are written already, all we need to do now is simply duplicate the Dropper1 (Ctrl-D) and move it to where you want it to be.

Name this Dropper Dropper2. You don't need to write a new Script, because it already has one from Dropper1. All you need to change is the Values inside the Config folder. I will change my Cooldown to 4 and Value to 12.

An Upgrader

Every tycoon needs an Upgrader, which increases the Value of Parts that pass through it. Create an upgrader model, or you can use this one:

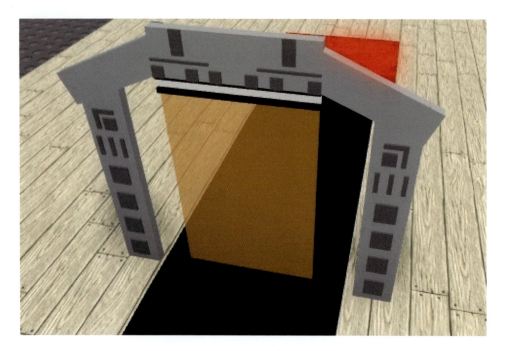

(I'm not the best at creating Models, if you want to use this, feel free to: https://www.roblox.com/library/2177444655/Tycoon-Upgrader)

Make sure that the upgrader Part is named Upgrade and has the CanCollide property set to false. In the picture above, the orange Part is the Upgrade and has CanCollide unchecked in the Properties panel.

Name the upgrader Model Upgrader1. If you don't have a Model, select all the Parts that you want included in your upgrader and press Ctrl-G to group, and name it Upgrader1. Move Upgrader1 into the Purchases Folder and duplicate one of the buttons to use for the upgrader. In the button, ensure that IsUpgrade is false, Object is Upgrader1, and Price is (insert reasonable price here e.g. 75).

Now insert an Script into the upgrader. Because an upgrader can be so versatile – multiplying value by 2, increasing by 5, dividing by 2 and increasing by 600, etc. – we will not have a Configuration folder this time. Instead, all values will need to be changed inside the Script itself.

```
local upgrade = script.Parent.Upgrade
upgrade.Touched:Connect(function(hit)
    local value = hit:FindFirstChild("Value")
    if value then
        value.Value = value.Value + 3
    end
end)
```

And with that simple Script that increments dropped Parts' `value`s by 3, you have successfully coded an upgrader.

By duplicating the upgrader and button and moving both to a new desired location, you can create another upgrader. Feel free to tweak the values as you wish.

Conveyor Walls

Conveyor walls are a simple yet overlooked part of tycoons. They can boost your moneymaking process by keeping in Parts that spilled out of the conveyor. Conveyor walls are simple to make.

The gray Parts around the conveyor are the conveyor walls.

What's more is that conveyor walls require no Script at all. You simply make them, name them ConveyorWalls1, put the Model into the Purchases folder, and make a button for it. That's it – that's all there is to making conveyor walls.

Dependencies

Play your game. Notice how all buttons appear on entry to your tycoon. What if you wanted to make a button invisible and unusable until a previous button was bought? Well, you can do so using dependencies.

Dependencies are StringValues that you insert into a button that signify what object to wait for before the button is purchasable. For example, if the button to buy Dropper2 has a dependency on Dropper1, then the button would not appear until Dropper1 is bought.

To begin using dependencies, insert a StringValue into the button to buy Dropper2, and name it Dependency. If you don't want to search through the Buttons folder, you can hold Alt and click on the button that you think is used to buy Dropper2. This will immediately select the button Part. Change the Value of Dependency to Dropper1. Then, open up the CoreScript once more. Make the following change.

```
local objects = {}
local guis = {}
local buttons = script.Parent:WaitForChild("Buttons")
local purchases = script.Parent:WaitForChild("Purchases")

for i,v in pairs(buttons:GetChildren()) do
    local obj = purchases:WaitForChild(v.Object.Value)
    objects[obj.Name] = obj:Clone()
    obj:Destroy()

    local txt = v.BillboardGui.TextLabel
    if v.IsUpgrade.Value then
        txt.Text = "Upgrade to "
    else
        txt.Text = "Buy "
    end

    txt.Text = txt.Text .. obj.Name .. ": $" .. v.Price.Value
    guis[#guis] = v.BillboardGui

    local dependency = v:FindFirstChild("Dependency")
    if dependency then
        script.Script:Clone().Parent = v
    end

    v.Touched:Connect(function(hit)
        local char = hit.Parent
        local plr = game.Players:GetPlayerFromCharacter(char)
        if plr then
```

What does this do? The additional part of the Script searches the button for a dependency. If there is one, it clones the Script inside the CoreScript and places it into the button.

Page 116

Insert a Script into the CoreScript. This will be the Script that makes the button fade in when the dependency is bought.

```lua
local dependency = script.Parent:FindFirstChild("Dependency")
local purchasedObjects = script.Parent.Parent.Parent:FindFirstChild("PurchasedObjects")

if dependency then
    local txt = script.Parent.BillboardGui.TextLabel

    script.Parent.Transparency = 1
    txt.BackgroundTransparency = 1
    txt.TextTransparency = 1
    script.Parent.CanCollide = false

    purchasedObjects:WaitForChild(dependency.Value)

    for i = 1, 20 do
        script.Parent.Transparency = script.Parent.Transparency - 0.05
        txt.BackgroundTransparency = txt.BackgroundTransparency - 0.05
        txt.TextTransparency = txt.TextTransparency - 0.05

        wait(0.05)
    end

    script.Parent.CanCollide = true
end
```

Try to see what these lines mean first.

Lines 5-10 make the button invisible. Line 12 waits until the **dependency** is bought, and the rest make the button fade in.

You may have noticed that even when the button is invisible, you can buy it if you walk over it with enough money. Let's fix that.

```lua
if hum.Health > 0 then
    local plrMoney = game.ServerStorage.PlayerMoney:FindFirstChild(plr.Name)
    if plrMoney.Value >= v.Price.Value then
        if v.CanCollide then
            objects[obj.Name].Parent = script.Parent.PurchasedObjects
            plrMoney.Value = plrMoney.Value - v.Price.Value

            for i = 1, 20 do
                v.Transparency = v.Transparency + 0.05
                txt.BackgroundTransparency = txt.BackgroundTransparency + 0.05
                txt.TextTransparency = txt.TextTransparency + 0.05

                wait(0.05)
            end

            v:Destroy()
        end
    end
end
```

That's it! You can now add dependencies to all the buttons you want. You can also add an option to upgrade the conveyor walls using dependencies. That's all there is to a tycoon.

Regenerating Tycoons

If you and a friend play your tycoon game (hypothetically, since you haven't shared it with other people... YET), you may notice that after a player leaves, the tycoon doesn't regenerate – meaning it doesn't clear the last player's tycoon progress. For example, if you buy the mine and leave the game, the next person to get your tycoon will see that the mine is already purchased – which we don't want. We want every player to have to build the tycoon from the ground up, which is why we need this Script. Insert a Script into ServerScriptService and name it RegenScript. Before editing, insert a Folder into the Workspace and move the tycoon Model inside. Name the Folder "Tycoons". Now open the Script and add the following code:

```lua
local tycoonBackups = {}
for index,tycoon in pairs(workspace.Tycoons:GetChildren()) do
    tycoonBackups[tycoon.Name] = tycoon:Clone()
end

game.Players.PlayerRemoving:Connect(function(plr)
    for index,tycoon in pairs(workspace.Tycoons:GetChildren()) do
        if tycoon.Owner.Value == plr then
            local backup = tycoonBackups[tycoon.Name]:Clone()
            tycoon:Destroy()
            wait()
            backup.Parent = workspace
        end
    end
end)
```

Congratulations! You have created a tycoon and completed this book. Using your knowledge, you can add even MORE to your tycoon – more walls, more droppers, upgraders, a duplicator, even a SECOND FLOOR! Or even a *third floor*! The possibilities are endless! If you went through this book in detail, then yo u should be well on your way to being a successful Roblox developer!

Oh, but wait – one final thing. When you want to share this game on Roblox, go to File in the upper right-hand corner, and then click on Publish to Roblox. Select (Create New), name it whatever you want, write a description, and set Privacy to Public. When you are finished editing the settings, click Create Place. Now you can share this tycoon with your friends.

Oh, and one more thing. If you want to create multiple tycoons, simply copy the Tycoon #1 model and paste it around your map. Then, people will be able to claim tycoons – one person each, however. You might like to rename your tycoons to Tycoon #2 and Tycoon #3. But other than that, that's it!

Printed in Poland
by Amazon Fulfillment
Poland Sp. z o.o., Wrocław